His Heart His Voice

Words of Encouragement

by Linda Daniels

© Copyright 2017 by Linda Daniels

ISBN 13: 978-0-692-92845-5

All rights reserved. This book is protected by the copyright laws of the United States of America. This book may not be copied or reprinted for commercial gain or profit. No portion of this book may be reproduced, stored in a retrieval system, or transmitted in any form or by any means—electronic, mechanical, photocopy, recording, scanning, or other—except for brief quotations in critical reviews or articles, without the prior written permission of Linda Daniels.

Published by Turning Page Books

Editorial assistance by Mike Yorkey

Cover and interior design by Blue Muse Studio

To contact Linda Daniels, order bulk copies, or invite her to speak, please contact her at sosgodskisses@gmail.com.

Table of Contents

Introduction 7
1. Taste the Lord. 10
2. Celebrate 12
3. Faithful 14
4. Pleasing God. 16
5. Take Time 18
6. Work Heartily. 20
7. Atmosphere. 22
8. The Secret Place. 24
9. Where Are Your Eyes?. 26
10. His Goodness. 28
11. Vessels 30
12. Flawless Word 32
13. Look to Him. 34
14. God's Love 36
15. Power in the Word 38
16. Breathe In 40
17. Rejoice 42
18. Light 44
19. A Trustworthy God 46
20. What You Know 48
21. Fresh. 50

22. Remember Who You Are 52
23. His Encouragement 54
24. Your Countenance 56
25. Worthy 58
26. Words 60
27. Your Stability 62
28. Friend 64
29. Trust 66
30. What Do You Value? 68
31. His Faithfulness 70
32. Three Things 72
33. Look to Me 74
34. Trials 76
35. There Is No One 78
36. The More I See You 80
37. All Things 82
38. Thankfulness Brings Joy 84
39. Stand for Righteousness 86
40. Sunshine 88
41. Stay True 90
42. A Tree 92
43. Seek the New 94
44. Simple 96
45. Standing on His Promises 98
46. Snuggle In 100
47. Seeds 102
48. His Presence 104
49. Resist Fear 106
50. A Glimpse of Him 108
51. Rejoice in the Lord 110
52. Preach Jesus 112
53. True Peace 114
54. Overpowering Love 116

55. My Yoke Is Light 118
56. He Never Changes 120
57. My Word 122
58. He Is Love 124
59. Roots 126
60. Sing 128
61. Our Words 130
62. My Peace 132
63. Name Above All Names 134
64. A Mountain 136
65. Moments 138
66. Bless the Lord Your God 140
67. Live in the Now 142
68. Look Beyond 144
69. Loads of Benefits 146
70. Live, Move, and Be 148
71. Lie Back 150
72. Cast Away 152
73. Carry One Another 154
74. Bible Stories 156
75. Change 158
76. Listen 160
77. Jesus Is 162
78. Influence Our Culture 164
79. Jehovah Jireh 166
80. I Am Your God 168
81. His Waves 170
82. Do Not Fear 172
83. I Have a God 174
84. A Cheerful Heart 176
85. Jealous 178
86. Your All-in-All 180
87. His Mercy 182

88. Our Heritage	184
89. He Keeps Us	186
90. Our God	188
91. Grace	190
92. He Delights in Me	192
93. Ashes	194
94. God's Abundance	196
95. Get in the Word	198
96. A Covering	200
97. Happy Feet	202
98. Glory in Me	204
99. God of Comfort	206
100. Extend Grace	208
101. Claim the Promises	210
102. Moment-by-Moment God	212
103. Examine Yourself	214
104. Don't Wait	216
105. Every Day	218
106. Enriched	220
107. Encourage Yourself	222
108. Empty Things	224
109. Come Away	226
110. Comfort Others	228
111. Rich Cream	230
112. Chosen	232
A Closing Thought by Senior Pastor Dave Olson	234
About the Author	235
Invite Linda Daniels to Speak Today	236

Introduction

About six years ago, our church had a guest speaker who taught us how to hear God's voice. Part of his teaching was his advice to keep a daily journal of what God said to us. I began to journal that day and have continued to do so. A fresh Word from the Father every day!

Three years ago, one of my daughters called to tell me that she kept seeing in her mind a picture of me writing—not children's books, which I had been attempting, but instead a book about spiritual matters.

One day, at church, my pastor approached me. He had met that week with some spiritual leaders from the area. They had been discussing how the Church could impact the local schools. All through the meetings, he saw a picture of me writing something to teachers, something that involved computers. He couldn't get that picture out of his mind.

Actually, I had been entertaining the idea of writing a weekly note of encouragement to teachers. Shortly after that, I began writing "God's Kisses" and would send my notes of encouragement every Monday morning via personal email. I started with six teachers, which quickly grew to about forty. I have been sending these emails out for over five years.

Some teachers began asking if I would consider publishing a book of these messages. I held that thought and pondered their counsel over time. I reflected on the times God had given me words for specific teachers at school. If those teachers shared that word with friends, their friends were touched also, even when the Word was not directed toward them. I began to realize that God's Word is always of benefit. His Word is His Word—bringing comfort, encouragement, peace, and direction. That drove me to the conclusion that if a few could be blessed by "God's Kisses," then many more would be blessed by a book that could be accessed by everyone, not just teachers.

I chose the title, *His Heart, His Voice,* because these are the two ways that I receive words from Him. Sometimes a word or "theme" comes into my mind. It comes frequently and with persistence until I realize that I am hearing God's heart concerning a matter. As I begin meditating on the Word He has given me, His thoughts soon grow into a message, along with Scripture to back it up.

The second way I hear from God is simply by asking Him what He wants to say to me. What do I need to hear? As He begins to speak, I write down what He says to me as I receive it—what I call a "fresh Word" from God. He then drops Scripture into my mind so that everything can be measured by His Word.

Please note that the verses God has given me or the words God has spoken to me are in boldface type throughout this book. Also, please note that I am using the New King James Version (NKJV) for Scripture verses, unless otherwise noted.

Each message is followed by a blank page on which you, the reader, can write your thoughts or prayers. My heart's desire is that you, too, will begin to hear His voice and start writing your own journal in this book.

There are no divisions in *His Heart, His Voice* according to topics. Many of the messages cross over more than one subject. I trust you to dog-ear or mark in some way those messages that especially speak to you. I would consider this book a success if the pages were marked, written upon, and well-worn.

I pray that *His Heart, His Voice* will encourage and inspire, and that it would be a launching pad for your own journal as you receive from His heart and His voice.

—Linda Daniels

My Life Scripture

O God, You are my God;
Early will I seek You;
My soul thirsts for You;
My flesh longs for You
In a dry and thirsty land
Where there is no water.
So I have looked for You in the sanctuary,
To see Your power and Your glory.
Because Your lovingkindness is better than life,
My lips shall praise You.
Thus, I will bless You while I live;
I will lift up my hands in Your name.
My soul shall be satisfied as with marrow and fatness,
And my mouth shall praise You with joyful lips.

Psalm 63:1-5

1
Taste the Lord

One of my favorite portions of Scripture is Psalm 34. There are so many promises! For instance, God will deliver us from trouble. He takes care of our needs. He will teach us and guard us. This is my favorite verse:

> ***Oh, taste and see that the Lord is good;***
> ***Blessed is the man who trusts in Him.***
> **PSALM 34:8**

When a child finishes a portion of his favorite food, he or she will probably say, "More, please!" That's how I feel about the Lord. I have tasted, and I want more.

The more I experience God's presence, the hungrier I get. I can never get enough of Him. I think this is a time when gluttony is allowed!

The Lord also wants to feed us with His Word. Seek His presence and spend time in His Word. You will soon find your hunger building. He loves it when His children say, "More, Lord!"

> ***For He satisfies the longing soul,***
> ***And fills the hungry soul with goodness.***
> **PSALM 107:9**

> ***Blessed are those who hunger***
> ***and thirst for righteousness,***
> ***for they shall be filled.***
> **MATTHEW 5:6**

2
Celebrate

Celebrate this day!

Celebrate life!

Celebrate loving and being loved!

Celebrate God's presence in your life!

Be thankful for His goodness and His grace. Dwell on the blessings of God. Let that determine your attitude for the day. He is Almighty God who rules the universe, yet He is concerned with every little detail of our days. He goes before us and prepares the way. Hallelujah!

Draw on Him today and rejoice for He is your salvation!

Praise the Lord, call upon His name;
Declare His deeds among the peoples,
Make mention that His name is exalted.
Sing to the Lord,
For He has done excellent things;
This is known in all the earth.
Cry out and shout, O inhabitant of Zion,
For great is the Holy One of Israel in your midst!

Isaiah 12:4b-6

Oh come, let us sing to the Lord!
Let us shout joyfully to the Rock of our salvation.
Let us come before His presence with thanksgiving;
Let us shout joyfully to Him with psalms.
For the Lord is the great God,
And the great King above all gods.

Psalm 95:1-3

3
Faithful

There is not a moment in time when I am not with you. There is never a shift in My feelings toward you. There will never be a time when I leave My throne or abdicate My authority. Therefore, I am always with you, loving you, and working on your behalf. Your part is to just lean back, rest in Me and trust. I have it. I have it. You will not need to "get over it"; you will be "carried" over it.

He is truly our Rock, our faithful God. The enemy would like us to feel lonely and vulnerable. He wants us to doubt. He wants us to worry and fret. Remember, he came to steal, kill, and destroy. But *God!* The enemy was defeated at Calvary. We live as children of the King. He is a wonderful Father who speaks love and life into us. Hallelujah!

*He who calls you is faithful,
who also will do it.*
1 THESSALONIANS 5:24

The Lord will reign forever and ever.
EXODUS 15:18

*For He Himself has said,
"I will never leave you nor forsake you."*
HEBREWS 13:5B

4
Pleasing God

*Therefore we make it our aim . . .
to be well pleasing to Him.*
2 Corinthians 5:9

A dear friend of mine and I were discussing how much we want to please the Lord. Not just to be obedient, but to truly bring Him pleasure by the things we say and do. We want to feel His smile on our lives. When we truly love someone, don't we try to do special little things to make that person happy and pleased? Doing so brings us joy as well.

Whom do you want to please? Your family? Your friends? Yourself? Those in authority? The world?

It sometimes goes against our nature to strive to please God because it might mean we are not pleasing our friends or our family. We might reject the world's view on particular issues. We may not participate in activities that we feel would not please the Lord. We might "stick out." We may make others feel uncomfortable about their own lifestyle.

What are you willing to risk to bring pleasure to the Lord, the one who is the lover of your soul?

*How precious is Your lovingkindness, O God!
Therefore the children of men put their trust under the shadow of Your wings.
They are abundantly satisfied with the fullness of Your house.
And you give them drink from the rivers of Your pleasures.*
Psalm 36:7-8

I choose to trust Him and please Him. I want to drink from the rivers of His pleasures!

5
Take Time

Take time for Me. Set aside a portion of your day for Me. I am jealous for your company. Come into the secret place.

Friends spend time together. They communicate their joys, disappointments, triumphs, and failures. They encourage, support, comfort, and, sometimes, redirect. They do it all out of a love for each other. So it is with Me. We need to meet often. We need to hear one another's voice. We need to share our hearts, our thoughts, and concerns.

In a short time, I can pour into you peace, joy, strength—anything that is needed. The longer you rest in My presence, the more I am able to impart to you. Read My Word as you would a dear friend's letter, listening for the voice of the one you love.

In the days ahead, you will need all that you have received from Me in order to stand. You will need to know how to meet with Me in the secret place. Come now into My chamber and sup with Me.

In John 15:15, Jesus calls his disciples "friends" and says that He will make known to them everything that He has heard from the Father. I want that! I want fresh revelation that only comes from the Lord. Everything we need to live a life that is pleasing to God is at our fingertips, if only we come to the Father.

> *... they should seek the Lord, in the hope that they might grope for Him and find Him, though He is not far from each one of us; for in Him we live and move and have our being.*
> **Acts 17:27-28**

6
Work Heartily

*Whatever may be your task,
work at it heartily (from the soul),
as (something done) for the
Lord, and not for men.*
COLOSSIANS 3:23 (Amplified Bible)

One Saturday afternoon, I was feeling tired and looking at a pile of school work before me. It was piled neatly on my kitchen island, in order of importance. I truly just wanted to push it aside and read a good book. This Scripture, however, brought me back to the task before me. I truly believed that God put me in my teaching position. Therefore, I was working to please Him, even if it was something as menial as running off papers or sharpening pencils. To God, nothing is unimportant. It all fulfilled the assignment that had been given to me.

So, what about this "heartily" thing? It's not just doing your best, but it's doing everything with a right attitude. For instance, how do you react when none of the copiers at work are functioning? When a co-worker is being less than cooperative? When you have to work extra hours? The flesh crawls in quite quickly if you're not careful, and makes you want to mumble, complain, and get grouchy. Doing the work is difficult at times, but keeping your attitude in check is even harder. So what can you do? Look to Him.

He is your steady anchor. Think of what a good God you have. Don't you want to please the One who loves you so? He will give you the strength each day to do the tasks set before you.

*You will keep him in perfect peace,
Whose mind is stayed on You,
Because he trusts in You.*
ISAIAH 26:3

7
Atmosphere

How is the atmosphere in your classroom? Your workplace? Your office? Your home? Do you feel peace? Do you feel the presence of God? Is He invited? Are you praying for your students, your co-workers, your family? God expects us to affect the atmosphere, wherever we are. When we carry Him, it is a normal occurrence.

Before the school year started, I used to anoint my classroom and my desks. I prayed over each desk before I knew who would be sitting there. You can pray over your workspace as well. You can pray over each room in your house, and you can pray over the businesses you enter.

You are His hand extended. You can create a safe haven, a place where others feel peace, love, and acceptance. Can you do this easily? Not in the natural, but with God, all things are possible. Yeah!

I encourage you to strengthen yourself in the Lord, and carry Him wherever you go. Let *Him* be the atmosphere.

> *You will keep him in perfect peace*
> *Whose mind is stayed on You,*
> *Because he trusts in You.*
> *Trust in the Lord forever,*
> *For in YAH, the Lord, is everlasting strength.*
> **Isaiah 26:3-4**

> *Give ear to my words, O Lord,*
> *Consider my meditation.*
> *Give heed to the voice of my cry,*
> *My King and my God,*
> *For to You I will pray.*
> *My voice You shall hear in the morning, O Lord;*
> *In the morning I will direct it to You,*
> *And I will look up.*
> **Psalm 5:1-3**

8
The Secret Place

Come away with Me. Come away, My beloved, away from what your eyes see and your ears hear in this world. Come into My secret place.

What is the secret place? It is not a place in the physical, with walls and a door that opens and shuts. It is a place in the spiritual realm.

This place is created when you seek Me and My presence with a desperate and hungry heart. In essence, you come into My chamber to sup with Me, the lover of your soul. It is a sweet place of communion and a place of safety from the world around you. It is a place where you can concentrate on what you *know*. The more you know Me, the easier it is to enter the secret place. The more you enter the secret place, the more you know Me.

> *For in the time of trouble*
> *He shall hide me in His pavilion;*
> *In the secret place of His tabernacle*
> *He shall hide me:*
> *He shall set me high upon a rock.*
> **Psalm 27:5**

> *Oh, how great is Your goodness,*
> *Which you have laid up for those who fear You,*
> *Which You have prepared for those who trust in You*
> *In the presence of the sons of men!*
> *You shall hide them in the secret place of Your presence.*
> **Psalm 31:19-20a**

> *He who dwells in the secret place of the Most High*
> *Shall abide under the shadow of the Almighty.*
> **Psalm 91:1**

9
Where Are Your Eyes?

Where are your eyes? Are they on the things of this world? Are they on the circumstances that you're currently facing? Are you looking to man for help? Are you looking inward for a reason or for a resolution?

Turn your eyes on Me, the One who loves you and upholds you. Let Me hold your gaze, and in turn, I will pour into you a fresh revelation of Myself, bringing peace, wisdom, and strength.

No one knows you like I know you. No one loves you like I love you. Be so "wrapped up" in Me that the momentary troubles of this life fade in importance, and your relationship with Me comes to the forefront. I will never forsake you. I am a faithful God.

What an amazing God we have. He is truly beautiful to behold!

> *I will lift up my eyes to the hills—*
> *From whence comes my help?*
> *My help comes from the Lord,*
> *Who made heaven and earth.*
>
> *He will not allow your foot to be moved;*
> *He who keeps you will not slumber.*
> *Behold, He who keeps Israel*
> *Shall neither slumber nor sleep.*
>
> *The Lord is your keeper;*
> *The Lord is your shade at your right hand.*
> *The sun shall not strike you by day,*
> *Nor the moon by night.*
>
> *The Lord shall preserve you from all evil;*
> *He shall preserve your soul.*
> *The Lord shall preserve your going out and your coming in*
> *From this time forth, and even forevermore.*
> **PSALM 121:1-8**

> *Unto You I lift up my eyes,*
> *O You who dwell in the heavens.*
> **PSALM 123:1**

10
His Goodness

*I would have lost heart, unless I had believed
That I would see the goodness of the Lord
In the land of the living.*
Psalm 27:13

I am overwhelmed by the goodness of God. How marvelous that we have not only an all-knowing, all-powerful God, but on top of that, *He is good.*

There is none like Him. All that He does flows out of His goodness. Even when things don't seem to be going our way, *He is good.*

Even if our finances seem to be going down the tube, *He is good.*

Even if we lose a loved one, *He is good.*

Our circumstances don't define who God is. He is always good. It is His character. That is why we trust Him.

*But You, O GOD the Lord,
Deal with me for Your name's sake;
Because Your mercy is good, deliver me.*
Psalm 109:21

I choose to trust in Him. I declare that He is good, regardless of my circumstances. I am thankful for the many blessings that flow out of His goodness.

11
Vessels

Over the last few years of teaching, I've had several difficult classes. Many days I felt inept, and on a few days, I wept out of sheer frustration.

I daily put on the armor of God, prayed over my room, asked the Holy Spirit to prepare the atmosphere, and prayed for my "heavy hitters."

Still, the battle raged. Then I had an "aha moment" with God when I read this section of Scripture:

> *But we have this treasure in earthen vessels,*
> *that the excellence of the power may be of God and not of us.*
> *We are hard-pressed on every side, yet not crushed; we are perplexed,*
> *but not in despair; persecuted, but not forsaken; struck down, but not destroyed—*
> *always carrying about in the body the dying of the Lord Jesus,*
> *that the life of Jesus also may be manifested in our body.*
> 2 CORINTHIANS 4:7-10

I got it. God just needed me to be available as a vessel so that His life might show through me. I needn't let myself be offended or let anger get the best of me. I should be looking for the greater purpose here. I should be showing Jesus. I should be showing the kind of love that comes only from the Father.

The outcome is for the Lord to decide. I was just the servant He was using at that moment in those children's lives. I may never see the fruit of seeds planted, but that's all right because I trust Him. I also know that He is always doing a work in me, fine-tuning me for His purposes.

I repented of my mumbling and grumbling and became determined to walk worthy of Him no matter the circumstances, for I represent Him.

I share this with you because we all walk this world as His ambassadors. We carry Him. What a joy and privilege!

> *For our light affliction, which is but for a moment,*
> *is working for us a far more exceeding and eternal weight of glory.*
> 2 CORINTHIANS 4:17

12
Flawless Word

Psalm 12 is concerned with the oppression of the poor and needy. The Lord says He will arise and set them in safety. Then verse 6 says:

> *The words of the Lord are pure words,*
> *Like silver tried in a furnace of earth,*
> *Purified seven times.*
> **PSALM 12:6**

This Scripture lets us know that when God says something, we can trust Him 100 percent. His word is pure.

We all know people who say one thing but do another. On the other hand, there are people who always speak truthfully. We say that their word is as good as gold. But God's words are pure as silver that has been purified seven times in the furnace. We can trust His word.

There was protection for the people because God said there would be. His Word continues to offer us protection today.

> *As for God, His way is perfect;*
> *The word of the Lord is proven.*
> *He is a shield to all who trust in Him.*
> **PSALM 18:30**

> *Put on the whole armor of God, that you may be able to stand against the wiles of the devil . . . And take the helmet of salvation, and the sword of the Spirit, which is the word of God.*
> **EPHESIANS 6:11, 17**

God's Word keeps us from sin. Consider these verses:

> *Your word I have hidden in my heart,*
> *That I might not sin against You.*
> **PSALM 119:11**

> *Direct my steps by Your word;*
> *And let no iniquity have dominion over me.*
> **PSALM 119:133**

Great peace have those who love Your law,
And nothing causes them to stumble.
Psalm 119:165

Let the pure word of God protect and guide you this day.

13
Look to Him

Do not be weary. Do not lose hope. Have I ever left you? Have I ever disappointed you? Am I a liar? I am always working in your life.

Trust Me. My timing will be perfect. You will see. You will rejoice. You will be glad, for I reign over all people and all circumstances. Lift your head and your heart, and fasten your eyes on Me.

We can all get frustrated waiting for our prayers to be answered, for situations to be resolved, for relationships to be restored. I welcome this word of encouragement from the Lord.

We need to lock eyes with Him and remember all the times that He has intervened in our lives. Doing so will build our faith and strengthen our resolve.

If you are one who is waiting, don't give up. Remember that while you wait, God is building something inside of you. Whatever that is, it will please God and be of benefit to you.

Wait and trust Him. He is a good, good God.

Why are you cast down, O my soul?
And why are you disquieted within me?
Hope in God, for I shall yet praise Him
For the help of His countenance.
Psalm 42:5

Truly my soul waits for God;
From Him comes my salvation.
He only is my rock and my salvation;
He is my defense;
I shall not be greatly moved.
Psalm 62:1-2

14
God's Love

I am lovesick for my God! My heart longs for His presence! These verses in the Amplified Bible express very well what I experience with my God. I pray that you experience God in this way also:

> *May Christ through faith [actually] dwell (settle down, abide, make his permanent home) in your hearts! May you be rooted deep in love and founded securely on love, That you may have the power and be strong to apprehend and grasp with all the saints [God's devoted people, the experience of that love] what is the breadth and length and height and depth (of it); [That you may really come] to know [practically, through experience for yourselves] the love of Christ, which far surpasses mere knowledge [without experience]; that you may be filled [through all your being] unto all the fullness of God [may have the richest measure of the divine Presence, and become a body wholly filled and flooded with God Himself]!*
> **Ephesians 3:17-19 (Amplified Bible, Classic Edition)**

Amen! Amen! Amen!

Enjoy His love today.

Be filled to overflowing.

Leave footprints of His love everywhere you go.

15
Power in the Word

There is power in My Word. Nehemiah read the Word to the people of Israel. They were moved, not only to repent, but to take action.

My Word can do the same for you. It can change you. My Word can uplift you, move you to tears, or inspire you to act. My Word will accomplish My purposes in you. What you must do is read My Word, digest My Word, and let it become a part of you. It is the Living Word. It grows in you and brings a new understanding and a deeper revelation of Me.

A section of Scripture can mean one thing to you the first time you read it, and later, you are struck by a whole new understanding. That is because I know what insight you need and when you need it. The Holy Spirit directs your understanding.

My Word is My gift to you. Without it, you can never reach your full potential. Feed on My Word, and be satisfied.

We need the nourishment of His Word on a daily basis. Fit reading the Bible into your schedule each day, and you will develop a new habit. Reading the Bible will become one of those habits that you will not want to break.

The Word is like a treasure chest that you don't have to search for. The treasure is right there for you. Become rich in His Word.

> *Your Word is a lamp to my feet*
> *And a light to my path.*
> **Psalm 119:105**

> *Open my eyes, that I may see*
> *Wondrous things from Your law.*
> **Psalm 119:18**

16
Breathe In

Breathe in.
    Relax.
        Release.
            Breathe in.
                Relax.
                    Release.
                        Breathe Me in.

Let My presence soothe and calm you.

Then relax and release your burdens to Me. Don't let worries and fears pull you down. I am here to walk you through the situations that cause you concern or fear. The enemy would love to see you fall apart, but you have Me.

Not only will I carry your burdens, but I will carry *you*.

We can get ourselves in such a tizzy when we allow our focus to stray from the Lord. Then the enemy makes it seem like our problems are insurmountable, and in our minds, they seem to multiply, getting bigger and bigger.

When you allow yourself to react in this way, it's like saying that God is not able to take care of you.

That is a lie from the pit. Rather, you need to face each obstacle in life with complete trust in the One who loves you like no other. You need to focus on all of His promises. You need to remember who He is, and who you are in His eyes.

He will not leave us or forsake us. That's a promise to stand on.

For He Himself has said," I will never leave you nor forsake you."
HEBREWS 13:5B

The Lord is my rock and my fortress and my deliverer;
God of my strength, in whom I will trust;
My shield and the horn of my salvation,
My stronghold and my refuge;
My Savior . . .
2 SAMUEL 22:2-3

17
Rejoice

Let Me overwhelm you with joy. Let Me overwhelm you with My grace and peace. Most of all, let Me overwhelm you with My love. Let Me be the answer to your trials, your hurts, your doubts. I am the one true God. Rejoice in My presence this day.

I am in awe of the goodness of our God. I am overwhelmed in His glorious presence!

For you are our glory and joy.
1 Thessalonians 2:20

But You, O Lord, are a shield for me,
My glory, and the One who lifts up my head.
Psalm 3:3

But God demonstrates His own toward us,
in that while we were still sinners, Christ died for us.
Romans 5:8

18
Light

I am Light. In Me there is no darkness. I clarify, I lift, I brighten, I show the way. I reveal. I can give courage when it seems dark. I shine on My beloved. You carry My light wherever you go. Brighten your world by allowing My light to shine forth. Don't hide it. Rather, be an encouragement to those whose path you cross today.

"Through the tender mercy of our God,
With which the Dayspring from on high has visited us;
To give light to those who sit in darkness and the shadow of death,
To guide our feet into the way of peace."
LUKE 1:78-79

Unto the upright there arises light in the darkness;
He is gracious, and full of compassion, and righteous.
PSALM 112:4

Then Jesus spoke to them again, saying,
"I am the light of the world. He who follows Me
shall not walk in darkness, but have the light of life."
JOHN 8:12

19
A Trustworthy God

Has God given you dreams concerning the future? Has He given you promises that are yet to be fulfilled?

In this world of "instant" everything, from text messaging to mobile maps, we find ourselves struggling while waiting for anything, including God. But we need to wait for God's timing.

I often remind myself that even though I have a dream and promises from God, I must admit that I can't figure out how it's all going to happen, even though I trust Him. So I need to wait.

As I was reading His Word, I came across this verse which encouraged me:

> *The Lord will perfect that which concerns me;*
> *Your mercy, O Lord, endures forever;*
> *Do not forsake the works of Your own hands.*
> **PSALM 138:8**

God will not let His plans or purposes fail you. Neither is He a "halfway" God. He will keep working until everything is perfected.

Maybe He sees that you're not ready for the dream. He might be preparing you from the inside out in order to be ready to handle whatever He has planned for you. Maybe other circumstances beyond your knowledge or control need to be lined up first.

The bottom line is this: Do you trust Him? Only He can make the circumstances and timing perfect for you and for me. I choose to believe that He continues to work on my behalf, and that He is true to His promises.

> *I will cry to God Most High, who performs on*
> *my behalf and rewards me [Who brings to pass*
> *His purposes for me and surely completes them]!*
> **PSALM 57:2 (Amplified Bible, Classic Edition)**

God made His chosen people wait to inherit their land after their exodus from Egypt, even though it was His plan for them to have the Promised Land. He did not drive out the other inhabitants immediately because the Israelites were not ready to take over, as this Scripture indicates:

> *I will not drive them out from before you in one year,*
> *lest the land become desolate and the beasts*
> *of the field become too numerous for you.*
> *Little by little I will drive them out from before you,*
> *until you have increased, and you inherit the land.*
>
> **Exodus 23:29-30**

God is good.
God is trustworthy.
God wants the best for us.
We need to be patient and continue to say yes to His plans.

20
What You Know

Rejoice in what you know. Do not fret about the unknown. What do you know about Me? I am faithful. I am gracious. I am trustworthy. I am powerful, yet gentle. I am the source for your every need. I am good, and I am love. With Me, you will lack nothing.

I continue to sit upon the throne, from which I rule and reign over all. No matter who "rules" in your world, I rule supreme. I hold the reins, and I can change events and circumstances instantly.

Rest in Me, and through divine revelation, I will unveil those things which are, as yet, unknown to you.

We all have a lot of "unknowns" in our life. We all want to know everything right now. I'm thinking God knows what we can and cannot handle. Sometimes we don't need to know until the time is right.

Whenever I teach a new concept in math, my advice to the students is to start with what they know and build on that. One has to have a grasp on addition before plunging into multiplication. Without multiplication knowledge, division can't be learned.

"Precept upon precept," the Bible says. That applies to our relationship with God as well. Until we build a relationship with the Lord, it's hard to trust Him.

We learn about Him through His Word, a great place to begin. In fact, a few years ago, our family was going through a difficult time. Throughout that period, I seemed to live in the Book of Psalms.

God told me to underline every verse in that book that contained the word "trust." I underlined thirty-six uses of this key word.

What God was doing was revealing Himself to me, which is how we learn experientially. When we go through difficult times, His calm and peaceful presence comforts us. When we pray, we receive His answer. When we listen to testimonies from others about how God intervened in their lives, we're encouraged.

Put together, all of these create a foundation for trust.

Trust in the Lord with all your heart,
And lean not on your own understanding.
Proverbs 3:5

Commit your way to the Lord;
Trust also in Him,
And He shall bring it to pass.
Psalm 37:5

Behold, You desire truth in the inward parts,
And in the hidden part You will make me to know wisdom.
Psalm 51:6

21
Fresh

Some things are tightly wrapped up to keep them fresh—like bread, crackers, and chips. With My Word, it is the opposite. Unwrap and open up My Word, that it may breathe into you a freshness of spirit.

People once had to buy their groceries daily because they could not keep them fresh. There was no refrigeration. The same applies to My Word. You need to get it daily so it will stay "fresh" in your heart and mind.

Consider what old bread is like—hard, crusty, and stale. You become like that if you do not keep yourself in the Word daily. Your heart starts to harden, your values begin to be blurred, your influence on others is no longer godly. You become stale spiritually.

Come to Me daily. Let Me feed you with My Word.

Give me understanding, and I shall keep Your law;
Indeed, I shall observe it with my whole heart.
Make me walk in the path of Your commandments,
For I delight in it.
Psalm 119:34-35

I long for Your Word, Lord.
Feed my hunger!

22
Remember Who You Are

Remember who you are—sons and daughters of the most high God, fully equipped to do My bidding.

You're covered in a robe of righteousness and kissed with My grace and mercy. You are My army upon this earth. Walk with your head high, your every sense tuned to Me. Be strong in your faith, but keep your heart soft.

Let love carry you. You are to be set apart from the world, but you are to minister My love to the world. You have all authority as My children. Remember who you are.

We get so wrapped up in our daily grind that we forget who we are in His sight. What a privilege to be called one of His children! What a joy to minister in His name!

> *But you are a chosen generation, a royal priesthood,*
> *a holy nation, His own special people, that you may*
> *proclaim the praises of Him who called you*
> *out of darkness into His marvelous light.*
> **1 Peter 2:9**

23
His Encouragement

A few years ago, a fellow teacher was faced with life-changing news when she learned that her husband was diagnosed with cancer.

I knew they were people of faith and loved the Lord. As I prayed for them, God gave me this word of encouragement that can apply to anyone who is going through a difficult time:

Circumstances will always be with you. Some bring you up; others bring you down. Some seem to sway your whole life like a swinging bridge caught in a gust of wind. That is why you lean into Me. I am stability. I am peace. I am sweetness and light when things seem dark. I am stronger than anything that can come against you.

Lean back against Me, and breathe Me in. Let my presence bring a new peace to your spirit and a new strength to your very being.

> *O Lord, my strength and my fortress,*
> *My refuge in the day of affliction.*
> **JEREMIAH 16:19**

24
Your Countenance

When Moses descended from Mount Sinai, his face shone. The people were afraid to approach him, so he put a veil over his face. He had just met with Me. The glow on his face was My presence lingering upon him.

It can be the same with you, My beloved, when you meet with Me, away from distractions and the clamoring of others. Come to the mountain daily and receive fresh impartations from Me. You will be strengthened and prepared for each day. You will not only leave with a fresh outlook, but a fresh look on your countenance.

Others should see, by just looking at you, that you have been with the Father. There should be something different about you that attracts others. You carry Me.

There is a woman who attends our church. She was saved while she was in prison. Every Sunday, she is up front, worshipping the Lord.

I have noticed the change in her countenance from week to week. Her face has become lighter, softer, and more peaceful. She now glows as she worships the Lord.

What a testament of God's grace and great love! How can we *not* want to spend time with Him?

> *Now it was so, when Moses came down from Mount Sinai*
> *(and the two tablets of the Testimony were in Moses' hand*
> *when he came down from the mountain), that Moses did not*
> *know that the skin of his face shone while he talked with Him.*
> *So when Aaron and all the children of Israel saw Moses, behold,*
> *the skin of his face shone, and they were afraid to come near him.*
>
> *And whenever the children of Israel saw the face of Moses,*
> *that the skin of Moses' face shone, then Moses would put*
> *the veil on his face again, until he went in to speak with Him.*
> EXODUS 34:29-30,35

25
Worthy

We have such sweet times of worship at our church. God's presence is so amazing, which I love.

Often people cry out, "Worthy! Worthy! Worthy is the Lord!" I wholeheartedly agree with their declaration of praise. He is worthy!

One Sunday, on my way home, I began thinking of why we say God is worthy. Many think about what He has done for them in the past: prayers answered, accidents avoided, healings in the body, and increase in areas of their life. Those are wonderful examples, and we are truly thankful for God's hand moving on our behalf. I don't think, however, that is why He is worthy.

We cry "worthy" not just because of what He has done, but because of Who He is. Before anything was created, **God was.** He created the heavens and the earth. He didn't work hard and sweat at the brow. He "spoke" them into being, followed by the creation of plants, animals, and people.

He is God Almighty, Maker of heaven and earth. He is omnipotent (all-powerful), omniscient (all-knowing), and omnipresent (present everywhere all the time). To have a God such as this is amazing, but the best part is that He is good!

Because He is good, He is loving, forgiving, patient, protective, supportive, faithful, trustworthy, righteous, and gracious. If He did not do one more thing for us in this life, He would still be worthy of our praise. He will never change. He is steadfast. He is glorious.

He is the one true God.

Let all the earth fear the Lord;
Let all the inhabitants of the world stand in awe of Him.
For He spoke, and it was done;
He commanded, and it stood fast.
PSALM 33:8-9

Oh come, let us worship and bow down;
Let us kneel before the Lord our Maker,
For He is our God,
And we are the people of His pasture
And the sheep of His hand.
PSALM 95:6-7

26
Words

And in Lystra a certain man without strength in his feet was sitting, a cripple from his mother's womb, who had never walked. This man heard Paul speaking. Paul, observing him intently and seeing that he had faith to be healed, said with a loud voice, "Stand up straight on your feet!" And he leaped and walked.
ACTS 14:8-10

Two things jumped out at me when I read this portion of Scripture. First, Paul was observant and listening to Holy Spirit. Second, Paul didn't speak a "Dear God, please heal this crippled man" type of prayer for this man. Rather, he spoke with authority and healing occurred. A word of knowledge, a declaration of faith, and presto—healing. I love it!

We have such power in our words—words to uplift, inspire, heal, and affect change. Of course, God wants us to use the authority that He has given us to bless others.

I have found that as I'm growing in the Lord, I tend to declare things instead of praying. Why not? I'm finding that doing so brings results and builds my own faith as I see God at work. Sometimes we come to the Lord with a "poor beggar" mentality instead of coming to Him with a "child of the King" mindset.

We can encourage or discourage others by how we speak. I don't know about you, but I can speak in anger or frustration before listening to Holy Spirit. Not good! When we are we speaking into people's lives, let it be for good.

A man has joy by the answer of his mouth,
And a word spoken in due season, how good it is!
PROVERBS 15:23

Pleasant words are like a honeycomb,
Sweetness to the soul and health to the bones.
PROVERBS 16:24

27
Your Stability

Find your stability in Me. I tell you that nothing in this world will remain unchanged, living or non-living. There will always be fluctuation, ups and downs, ins and outs. Only I am steady and sure—the Rock on which you can lean. Don't think it is a sign of weakness to lean on Me. Rather, it is a sign of strength, of wisdom. When others around you are faltering, you have Me as your anchor. Only as you stand strong in Me can you be a help to others.

Jesus Christ is the same yesterday, today, and forever.
Hebrews 13:8

He is the Rock, His work is perfect;
For all His ways are justice,
A God of truth and without injustice;
Righteous and upright is He.
Deuteronomy 32:4

Thank you Lord for being our stability.

28
Friend

Have you ever forgotten a friend's birthday? Have you ever disappointed a friend by not showing up when expected?

It happens. We could blame our forgetfulness or inability to show up at the appointed time on circumstances, busyness, or old age. It doesn't matter what the reason or excuse is. Any time we forget something or don't do what we said we were going to do, we feel bad.

People are people and subject to frailties, mistakes, and forgetfulness. We are not perfect. As much as we want to depend on our friends or our family members, they let us down occasionally, and vice versa.

There is only *One* who will not let us down, who will not disappoint, who will not forget us. That Person is the Lord, who is our fast friend. In fact, He calls us "friends." He laid down his life for us, as His friends.

The Lord extends us grace moment by moment. He comforts and consoles us. He will never lie or deceive us. He always wants the best for us. He gives us wisdom and direction, and He upholds us. He carries us when we can't seem to make it on our own. He is our Rock. As the well-known hymn says, "What a friend we have in Jesus!"

Spend time with Him and communicate with Him. That is the best way to build a friendship.

"Greater love has no one than this, than to lay down one's life for his friends. You are My friends if you do whatever I command you. No longer do I call you servants, for a servant does not know what his Master is doing; but I have called you friends, for all things that I heard from My Father I have made known to you."
John 15:13-15

*God is not a man that He should lie,
Nor a son that He should repent.
Has He said, and will He not do?
Or has He spoken, and will He not make it good?*
Numbers 23:19

29
Trust

Our whole relationship with God is based upon trust. He is looking for us to lay everything at His feet, so He can freely work in our hearts and lives. We wouldn't have come to Jesus in the first place if we did not trust Him to forgive our sins and become our Lord and Savior.

Somewhere along the line, we begin to take back certain areas of our lives. For instance, instead of trusting the Lord for our finances, we fret and scheme to solve the precarious situation ourselves. We become filled with fear and worry.

Or, maybe we have a loved one who is in rebellion. We wring our hands, trying to control things ourselves, but when nothing happens, we become frustrated and angry. We forget that God loves that son, daughter, or family member more than we do, and He is much more capable of turning that person around than we are. After all, He turned us around at the point of salvation. Whatever our trial or their trials, God is bigger!

I would encourage you to turn to His Word whenever you feel a lack of trust in your heart. Build your faith by increasing your knowledge of Him.

For You have been a shelter for me,
A strong tower from the enemy.
I will abide in Your tabernacle forever;
I will trust in the shelter of Your wings.
PSALM 61:3-4

"But whoever listens to Me will dwell safely,
And will be secure, without fear of evil."
PROVERBS 1:33

"Therefore do not worry, saying, 'What shall we
eat?' or 'What shall we drink?' or 'What shall we wear?'
For after all these things the Gentiles seek. For your heavenly
Father knows that you need all these things. But seek
first the kingdom of God and His righteousness,
and all these things will be added to you."
MATTHEW 6:31-33

> *"Behold, God is my salvation,*
> *I will trust and not be afraid;*
> *For YAH, the Lord, is my strength and song;*
> *He also has become my salvation."*
> **Isaiah 12:2**

30
What Do You Value?

What do you value? God brought this question to mind as I was watching the teachers on my 4th grade team interact with one another. Witnessing the way they cared for each other brought tears to my eyes because I was reminded of how much I loved and valued them as friends and as teammates.

On the way home, I thought of what it meant to value someone you know well or something you cherish. If you have something valuable, you appreciate it. You go out of your way to protect and preserve it, especially when it comes to relationships. I'm sure we would all put our family members in the valued category, along with close friends and even our pets.

Then there's stuff that we all value: the house, the shiny car, the nice jewelry, the big screen TVs, the season tickets, and the club membership. But wait a minute! That's a short list of monetary valuables, and those are things that don't truly satisfy in the long run.

So what should *we* value?

Actually, the question to ask ourselves is this: "What does *GOD* value?" If we take after God's own heart, we should value what He values. And what does He rate highly? These Scriptures are a good place to start:

> *You shall love the Lord your God with all your heart,*
> *with all your soul, and with all your strength.*
> **DEUTERONOMY 6:5**

> *" 'Honor your father and your mother,'*
> *and 'You shall love your neighbor as yourself.' "*
> **MATTHEW 19:19**

> *But He answered and said, "It is written,*
> *'Man shall not live by bread alone,*
> *but by every word that proceeds*
> *from the mouth of God.' "*
> **MATTHEW 4:4**

> *"You have loved righteousness and hated lawlessness;*
> *Therefore, God, your God, has anointed you*
> *With the oil of gladness more than your companions."*
> **HEBREWS 1:9**

He values our hearts committed to Him. He values families. He values mankind. He values His Word. He values righteousness. We show our love for Him by valuing the same things.

A verse that I'm meditating on in my own life is Psalm 119:37, which says:

> *Turn away my eyes from looking at worthless things,*
> *And revive me in Your way.*

I'd say that's a pretty good place to start and end.

31
His Faithfulness

I'm thankful that I live in an area where we have the four seasons and the changes they bring. I think of the One who created the seasons and their order. God set the seasons into motion and has been faithful to keep them. We can always trust that spring will follow winter, and summer will come after spring.

This is just one example of God's faithfulness. Think of the sun. Doesn't the sun come up every morning and set every evening? We expect that to happen because the sun has always risen in the east and set to the west. We glory in the sunlight that warms us and grows our crops and revel in the moon and stars we see every night. Again, the faithfulness of God reflected in His creation.

If you can trust God to be faithful in overseeing this vast universe, then you can trust Him to provide the everyday needs in your life. Just as He is faithful to sustain this world, He will be faithful to sustain you. If He has set something into motion for your life, He will be faithful to carry it out for His glory. You just need to trust and keep your eyes on Him.

What a glorious and mighty God we serve!

Then God said, "Let there be lights in the firmament of the heavens to divide the day from the night; and let them be for signs and seasons, and for days and years and let them be for lights in the firmament of the heavens to give light on the earth"; and it was so. Then God made two great lights; the greater light to rule the day, and the lesser light to rule the night. He made the stars also.
Genesis 1:14-16

Your faithfulness endures to all generations;
You established the earth, and it abides.
They continue this day according to Your ordinances,
For all are Your servants.
Psalm 119:90-91

Let the heavens rejoice, and let the earth be glad;
And let them say among the nations, "The Lord reigns."
1 Chronicles 16:31

Rejoice in the Lord today and know that He will sustain you.

32
Three Things

I want to remind you of three things:

1. All authorities have been established by God. We should show this in thought, word, and deed so as to please God.

> *Let every soul be subject to the governing authorities. For there is no authority except from God, and the authorities that exist are appointed by God.*
> **Romans 13:1**

2. We can do all things through Christ who strengthens us. In *all* things. Let yourself dream.

> *I can do all things through Christ who strengthens me.*
> **Philippians 4:13**

3. We have a good and gracious God! He is kind, loving, trustworthy, merciful, wise, and much, much more!

> *Oh, that men would give thanks to the Lord for His goodness, And for His wonderful works to the children of men!*
> **Psalm 107:8**

I would like to add this Scripture because it blesses me so much.

> *There is no one like the God of Jeshurun, Who rides the heavens to help you, And in His excellency on the clouds. The eternal God is your refuge, And underneath are the everlasting arms; He will thrust out the enemy from before you, And will say, "Destroy!"*
> **Deuteronomy 33:26-27**

Today's "super heroes" in the film world have nothing on God. He is the Almighty, and He fights on our behalf. Be encouraged!

> *What then shall we say to these things? If God is for us, who can be against us?*
> **Romans 8:31**

33
Look to Me

What seems large and insurmountable to you is nothing to me. One word spoken, one touch from Me, and it is done. Consider the parting of the sea, the plagues of Egypt that never touched My chosen ones, dry bones coming alive, covered with flesh and rising up.

With Me, nothing is impossible. Don't look at circumstances like the world does. Don't be crippled by fear. Use your faith and your spiritual senses. I am your God. Look to Me.

Life is always full of twists and turns. We can never plan well enough. We can never be problem-free. We do what we can, but some things are out of our control. Granted, not everyone's problems are of the same degree. Does it matter to God? Is anything too big or too small to take to Him in prayer? I think not.

Fear is our enemy, and we can't allow ourselves to be overwhelmed by it. Dwelling on a possible problem can bring that very problem into our lives. In the Old Testament, Job—who had a lot of problems—said this:

> *For the thing I greatly feared has come upon me,*
> *And what I dreaded has happened to me.*
> *I am not at ease, nor am I quiet;*
> *I have no rest, for trouble comes.*
> **JOB 3:25-26**

We need to be in the habit of giving everything to God—every moment, every day. Live in faith and trust. Instead of speaking about the things we fear, let's declare God's sovereignty, God's power, God's wisdom, God's love, and God's direction over us. Fear moves Satan's hands; faith moves God's hands.

> *For God has not given us a spirit of fear,*
> *but of power and of love and of a sound mind.*
> **2 TIMOTHY 1:7**

34
Trials

As I was thanking God for being such a good God, He gave Me this Word:

I most gladly pour out fresh anointings and fresh blessings upon My beloved. The trials bring spiritual growth, and My goodness solidifies that growth. Always look for My goodness in the midst of darkness. I am there. I am a faithful God who carries you and brings you out to a better place.

Everyone goes through trials. That's just a part of life. How you go through those trials depends on how much you trust God. He gives us all authority in His name.

He tells us He is the lifter of our heads (PSALM 3:3).

He surrounds us with favor as with a shield (PSALM 5:12).

He carries us when it seems we can't go one more step (ISAIAH 46:3-4).

He is our Shalom, our peace. (ISAIAH 26:3-4).

There are multiple promises and provisions found in His Word. We need to take Him at His Word. What He says in Scripture is our greatest weapon in times of trouble.

> *Fear not, for I am with you:*
> *Be not dismayed, for I am your God.*
> *I will strengthen you,*
> *Yes, I will help you,*
> *I will uphold you with*
> *My righteous right hand.*
> ISAIAH 41:10

35
There Is No One

There is no one who knows us like He does.
There is no one who loves us like He does.
There is no one who embraces us like He does.
There is no one who forgives us like He does.
There is no one who lifts us up like He does.
There is no one who fills us like He does.
There is no one who inspires us like He does.
There is no one who comforts us like He does.
There is no one who carries us like He does.
There is no one who protects us like He does.
There is no one who provides for us like He does.
There is no one who leads us like He does.
There is no one who whispers "sweet nothings" like He does.
There is no one who captures our hearts like He does.
There is no one like our God.

For I am God, and there is no other;
I am God, and there is none like Me.
ISAIAH 46:9B

36
The More I See You

I love the lyrics in a song by Sean Feucht in which he sings how the more he sees God, the more he loves Him.

The song's lyrics are simple but so profound when it comes to building relationships. Think about it: the more you are with a loved one, the deeper your love grows. The more you see that person, the more you want to be with him or her. On the other hand, if you spend less and less time with a person, the less you desire to be with him or her, and your love begins to wane.

So it is with the Lord. If you set your heart on Him, the deeper your love becomes. The more He reveals of Himself, the more you want to "see" Him and understand His heart. You develop your hunger by spending time with Him, by being in His Word, and by longing for a fresh revelation of Him. With God, there is always more—more love, more wisdom, more power, and more grace. The greater your hunger, the greater the blessings.

In Deuteronomy 33, Moses blesses the children of Israel before his death. I love what Moses says about Naphtali, the sixth son of Jacob and the founder of the Israelite tribe of Naphtali:

> *And of Naphtali he said:*
> *"O Naphtali, satisfied with favor,*
> *And full of the blessings of the Lord . . . "*
> **DEUTERONOMY 33:23A**

I want that said over me—that I was satisfied with favor and full of the Lord's blessings.

That's why I have set my heart on Him and set my eyes on Him. I want more, and you should desire that as well!

37
All Things

Some things in life are hard, some are tedious, some are not pleasant. Remember, I am with you in *all things*. I am the steady One when you are faltering. I am the strong One when you are weak. I am the One who carries you when it seems you cannot take another step.

If your child were to stumble, would you not catch him? If he were hurt, would you not soothe him? If he were lost, would you not show him the way? So it is with you. I am your loving Father—your Abba Daddy. I watch over you. I neither slumber nor sleep. You can lean on Me and trust Me to carry you through *all things*.

What an awesome God we have! He is always watching over us as a loving Father.

> *He will not allow your foot to be moved;*
> *He who keeps you will not slumber.*
> *Behold, He who keeps Israel*
> *Shall neither slumber nor sleep.*
> PSALM 121:3-4

38
Thankfulness Brings Joy

Thankfulness brings joy. It brings peace. Thankfulness opens the flow of blessings into your life. It is the key to living a full life, allowing My grace to flow easily over you. It draws you into My presence and brings fresh revelation of Me.

I received this Word on my way to church. I had been thinking of all the things in my life that I was thankful for. I decided to make a list of those things. Here's a sample from my list, which is probably similar to one you could make:

- My salvation
- My husband, children, and grandchildren
- My extended family
- My friends
- My church body
- Our jobs
- My co-workers
- Living in the United States
- Good health
- The faithfulness of God
- The coming of spring!
- Chocolate . . . and more chocolate

I could go on and on, but the point is that we often take so much for granted. We could give God thanks continually and still not keep up because He constantly showers us with His blessings.

Thankfulness brings us into His gates. When we are within His gates, we are in His presence. That's what we should all desire because to be in His presence is to experience the fullness of joy.

Enter His gates with thanksgiving,
And into His courts with praise.
Be thankful to Him, and bless His name.
PSALM 100:4

39
Stand for Righteousness

When you stand for righteousness, you are never alone, for I stand with you. Those who went before you applaud you from heaven. My angels surround you. Your reward is in My hand. Sometimes the temporary seems overwhelming and impossible, but I offer an eternity of blessings and a wealth of joy and peace. Those blessings begin here, right where you live, *right now*. Those warriors who stand in My camp will be honored by Me. I will open doors for you. I will put up walls of protection for you. I will show myself strong on your behalf.

So, gird up your loins, pick up your sword, and follow Me.

We do not live in a society where righteousness is honored. We are bombarded by the opposite of righteousness daily, sometimes even from those who claim to be Christians.

The theme seems to be, "If it makes you feel good, do it." This mantra is universal, regardless of who it hurts or influences. Are we using inappropriate language or laughing at lewd jokes? Are we more concerned with impressing the people around us than we are about pleasing the Lord?

Consider what Jesus did for us on the Cross. Was He concerned with how He looked to others? No, His heart was set toward us, the benefactors of His pain and suffering.

Now is a good time to re-examine ourselves in the light of Calvary. We need to live with a spirit of thankfulness for our freedom from sin and an overwhelming love for the One who gave it all for us, even while we were yet sinners.

I want to show my love for Him by living, moving, and breathing in Him. I want Him to be delighted in Me, for He is my delight.

> *And whatever you do, do it heartily, as to the Lord and*
> *not to men, knowing that from the Lord you will receive*
> *the reward of the inheritance; for you serve the Lord Christ.*
> **Colossians 3:23-24**

> *See that no one renders evil for evil to anyone,*
> *but always pursue what is good both for yourselves and for all.*
> *Rejoice always, pray without ceasing, in everything give thanks;*
> *for this is the will of God in Christ Jesus for you.*
> *Do not quench the Spirit. Do not despise prophecies. Test all things;*
> *hold fast what is good. Abstain from every form of evil.*
> **1 Thessalonians 5:15-22**

40
Sunshine

When my husband and I were in college, we had an older couple who invited us to their house often, where they would feed and love on us and our firstborn. Don and Marge were like our "parents away from home."

When I received the Lord as my Savior not long after meeting them, I felt comfortable enough to share my experience with Marge. She and her husband didn't go to church, and I don't think she knew the Lord. When I told Marge that I had become a believer in Christ, she told me that she had some relatives whose lives were centered on church and their faith. With a wistful look on her face, she said, "Their lives are like sunshine."

Hearing that phrase stirred something in me. After finishing college and moving on with our lives, we didn't keep in touch, but I've never forgotten what Marge said, and even more so, the look of longing on her face.

These days, there have been times when I've asked myself, "Would someone look at me and use the word 'sunshine' to describe me? Do I stir up a longing in people? Do I let the Son shine through me as I live and move and be?" I think those are questions we all need to ask ourselves.

Inside my home today, I have a tall glass container that holds a candle. I love how the light is reflected off the glass when the candle is lit. After a while, though, the glass becomes dulled and discolored by soot from the flame. My glass candle holder isn't as attractive, and the light isn't as bright.

When I notice the dull light, I remove the candle and give the container a good cleaning. Voila, and the light shines through again.

It's the same with us. If we allow what we might think are little indiscretions like poor attitudes, inappropriate language, or watching TV shows or movies that are not wholesome, our light becomes dull. We seem more like the world, and there is nothing about us that draws others to Christ. We lose the opportunity to lead others to Him.

I know we think of "This Little Light of Mine" as a Sunday school song for children, but the simple lyrics should be taken seriously by us. We should always be representing God and what He has placed in us. We can't let the " little things" ruin our testimony.

Instead, our lives should be like "sunshine."

Let your light so shine before men, that they may
see your good works and glorify your Father in heaven.
Matthew 5:16

Arise, shine;
For your light has come!
And the glory of the Lord is risen upon you.
Isaiah 60:1

41
Stay True

Do you have some vacation time coming up? Or how about a long holiday weekend? No matter how long your break, here is a Word for you.

Stay true to Me. Rest, relax, be refreshed, but do not forsake spending time with Me and My Word. As your tight schedule loosens, allow time to soak in My presence. Glean from every moment those things which I desire to impart to you. This season may allow you opportunities to travel, to see and speak with people you have never met before. Be ready to show *Me* through your words and actions. Be ready with an answer. Be ready to show love and kindness.

You will be recompensed for the time you spend doing kingdom work. You will be blessed with new strength, wisdom, and fortitude. No one can outgive Me, for I am a generous God. Seek Me.

God is so good! God is so generous!

Recently our pastor said, "God gives to an extravagant degree." Hallelujah! I'm so glad He does.

Now that I have a little more free time, I look forward to attending intercessory prayer times at my church. I want to spend more time with the Lord. Just think, He promises to bless us when we do things that our heart desires in the first place! How awesome is that?

Allow me to pray this verse of Scripture over you:

The grace of the Lord Jesus Christ, and the love of God,
and the communion of the Holy Spirit be with you all. Amen.
2 Corinthians 13:14

42
A Tree

Trees are lovely to behold. I like to sit on my deck and look at the three river birch trees we planted in our backyard. They are so pretty and provide peaceful shade. Watching the breeze stir them and listening to the leaves swish in the wind is relaxing.

While watching the glistening leaves move, I was reading some of my favorite verses concerning trees. God then placed these thoughts in my mind:

A tree stands tall and strong, producing fruit, providing shade and shelter. Its beauty and tranquility is wonderful to behold. A tree sends roots deep into the soil. Because of those roots, a tree is not easily moved. It holds on, even during battering storms. If a tree is cut down, it soon sends up shoots to begin new growth. There is a tenacity which I have placed in the tree. I have created it to be so.

As you live out your life, consider the tree. Be rooted in Me, standing tall and strong. Life's storms may buffet you and even break a few branches, but I am always your strength.

Produce the fruit of the Spirit, and walk out your faith in tranquility and tenacity. Display the beauty of the Lord.

Now consider these verses the Lord also gave me:

> *"Blessed is the man who trusts in the Lord,*
> *And whose hope is the Lord.*
> *For he shall be like a tree planted by the waters,*
> *Which spreads out its roots by the river,*
> *And will not fear when heat comes;*
> *But its leaf will be green,*
> *And will not be anxious in the year of drought,*
> *Nor will cease from yielding fruit."*
> JEREMIAH 17:7-8

> *But I am like a green olive tree in the house of God;*
> *I trust in the mercy of God forever and ever.*
> PSALM 52:8

43
Seek the New

"Do not remember the former things,
Nor consider the things of old.
Behold, I will do a new thing,
Now it shall spring forth;
Shall you not know it?
I will even make a road in the wilderness,
And rivers in the desert,
The beast of the field will honor Me,
The jackals and the ostriches,
Because I give waters in the wilderness
And rivers in the desert,
To give drink to My people, My chosen.
This people I have formed for Myself;
They shall declare My praise."

Isaiah 43:18-21

As I was meditating on this Word, God laid this on my heart:

Do not cling to past victories, to past moves of My Spirit. Those experiences with the Divine are intended to strengthen you, to build a foundation for your faith, to put a new boldness in you. Some of My people want to, in essence, worship those experiences and miss what I intended.

Do not be satisfied with the old, but seek the new. Always be looking for my heart, My intentions for you as My chosen. Let your eyes and ears be open so that you may receive fresh revelation and reach new heights. There is an abundance waiting for those who strain for a glimpse of Me, whose hearts grow hungrier and hungrier as the days pass. I am not a stagnant God. I am always moving, always building My kingdom through those who have laid down their lives in order to be attuned to Me. Be watching for a fresh movement. You don't want to miss it and be left lacking.

I believe it's important to remember all the things God has done in our lives but not "camp out" there. We should always want a fresh touch from Him. We should always want to walk in the "now" of God.

44
Simple

The simplest things are often the most profound. A smile at the right time, a pat on the shoulder, a hug, a word of encouragement. The grandiose can become cluttered with vanity, pride, intimidation. Be simple and straightforward.
In the same way, come to Me as a little child. Wide-eyed wonder, with no guile. I will tell you that I love you and you are Mine. That is the simple, yet profound truth.

As these words were spoken to me, I thought of how we all need that encouragement, especially when the stress level is high. We need to be sensitive to each other and build each other up with simple kindnesses.

Also, this Word is a good reminder that we can just be ourselves when we come to the Lord. He knows us inside and out anyway. Knowing that should give us a sense of peace and comfort.

*Let each of you look out
not only for his own interests,
but also for the interests of others.*
Philippians 2:4

*But the fruit of the Spirit is love, joy, peace, longsuffering,
kindness, goodness, faithfulness, gentleness,
self-control. Against such there is no law.*
Galatians 5:22-23

45
Standing on His Promises

Have you ever been given a Word from the Lord or had a dream in your heart that you believe was from Him? Are you still waiting for that dream or promise to be fulfilled? I know several people in that situation, including me. So what do we do?

Think about Joseph and his coat of many colors. Did he think that it was his destiny to be sold by his brothers and end up in prison?

Then there was Samuel. It took a while for him to step into his destiny. He had some growing up to do.

And David... he was anointed to be king long before that event actually happened. Did he have an easy time waiting for that fulfillment? No. Life was dangerous for him as he waited.

Did any of these men give up? Did they stop trusting God for the promise? No.

God's timing is never our timing. His ways are not our ways. Our part is to stand on God's Word and declare it to the heavens. If we believe that we have done everything we can, then we are tethering ourselves to His Word, His promise, and we can stand in faith.

God is not just trying to make us squirm during difficult patches, but He is preparing us so that we are ready for the promise. Do any of us need more faith? Yes. Do we need to learn patience? For sure. Do we need wisdom? Maturity? Direction? Of course.

All of these come from a loving God who doesn't want us to mess up because we are not ready. He always has our best interests in mind because He loves us so. We are His delight, the apple of His eye. How can we not trust Him? I choose to keep my eyes on Him, the author and finisher of our faith.

*Therefore, know that the Lord your God,
He is God, the faithful God who keeps covenant
and mercy for a thousand generations with those
who love Him and keep His commandments.*
Deuteronomy 7:9

He who calls you is faithful, who also will do it.
1 Thessalonians 5:24

*Let us hold fast the confession of our hope
without wavering, for He who promised is faithful.*
Hebrews 10:23

46
Snuggle In

Do you ever have those days when you don't handle things very well? Maybe you let your temper get the best of you, or perhaps you melted in a mess of tears.

I have to say I have reacted both of those ways in the past. Thankfully, God is so gracious and so encouraging. This is what He laid on my heart:

Snuggle down into Me, like a chick pushes under the soft feathers of mother hen's wing. Like a puppy pushes through the others in a litter to nestle against its mother, and to receive sustenance. I am your comforter, and I am your sustenance. I am your strength. As the strong winds of this life swirl around you, find Me in the lee of the storm. You are safe with Me. I see beyond your circumstances. I know the plans I have for you. Find peace in Me.

Then He gave me these verses:

*The Lord will be a refuge for the oppressed,
A refuge in times of trouble. And those who know Your
name will put their trust in You; For You, Lord,
have not forsaken those who seek You.*
PSALM 9:9-10

*How precious is Your lovingkindness, O God!
Therefore, the children of men put their
trust under the shadow of Your wings.*
PSALM 36:7

*For I know the thoughts that I think toward you,
says the Lord, thoughts of peace and not of evil,
to give you a future and a hope.*
JEREMIAH 29:11

47
Seeds

God has been talking to me about seeds. He desires to plant seeds in us—ideas, desires, anointings, and callings. Whatever He wants to grow in us is first started as a seed. As in the physical, there is often preparation before the seed is planted to assure growth. The "ground" needs to be prepared and is a necessary process that may not be pleasant, however.

First of all, the "old" needs to be exposed, turned over, and removed. Old "roots" that have caused us problems in the past and have stunted spiritual growth must be faced head-on. We have to trust our heavenly Father during this process, remembering that the rewards far outweigh the momentary discomfort.

I trust God to strip off the old and plant the new in me. I know He loves me and wants the best for me. It's like when a small child is told that Mom or Dad know best, even if it involves nasty things like shots or cavities being filled. We trusted our parents to take care of us. We should trust the Lord even more for He loves us so much.

I want God to remove everything that screams "me" and replace it with what says "Lord." I want His touch on my life, and I want to live worthy of whatever He chooses to pour into me. He is a good Abba Daddy, and He wants the best for us. Open yourself to Him today, and let Him do some "spring cleaning" and some "spring planting."

He shall be like a tree planted by the rivers of water,
That brings forth its fruit in its season,
Whose leaf also shall not wither;
And whatever he does shall prosper.

PSALM 1:3

48
His Presence

Come into My presence and sup with Me. Be nourished and strengthened. Be filled with joy. Experience My glory. Come away to the secret place and receive from Me. I will teach you precept upon precept. In My presence there is revelation. In My presence there is power. My presence is a well that refreshes and never goes dry. It is an intimate communion. No matter what is happening in the external, the inner man is fed, cleansed, wrapped in robes of My glory, and changed forever in My presence. Enter, My beloved.

Nothing compares to His presence.

One Sunday, I was ill and could not go to church. When I do go to church on Sunday morning, it's easy to be swept into His presence when the church body worships. I didn't want to miss that!

But God is faithful! I put on my music, lay before Him on my living room floor, and experienced His presence. Afterward, He gave me the Word above. I'm so thankful that He is as anxious to meet with us as we are to be with Him. It's like experiencing a taste of heaven here on earth! Hallelujah!

Set your eyes on Him, and ask for a taste of His presence, even as you go about your daily tasks or Sunday rest.

In Your presence is fullness of joy.
Psalm 16:11b

49
Resist Fear

As I received this Word, I sensed that there were some who really needed to hear these words. Even if this doesn't seem timely to you, it is a valuable Word that you can use to be encouraged.

Resist fear. It is not from Me. The enemy wants to see you cower, but I want to see you stand tall, wrapped in the shield of favor which I have given you. Know Me. Know My Word. Build up your arsenal for the days to come. Recall the moments in your life when I have intervened, and let that increase your faith. The enemy crawls on his belly as a snake. I ride the clouds in the heavenlies.

Keep that in perspective. Be at rest.

Remember who you are and whose you are. Rejoice in that, and watch fear slide away.

Sing to God, you kingdoms of the earth;
Oh, sing praises to the Lord,
To Him who rides on the heaven of heavens, which were of old!
Indeed, He sends out His voice, a mighty voice.
Ascribe strength to God;
His excellence is over Israel,
And His strength is in the clouds.
PSALM 68:32-34

For You, O Lord, will bless the righteous;
With favor You will surround him as with a shield.
PSALM 5:12

50
A Glimpse of Him

During worship and prayer time, I prayed for a woman who was dealing with loneliness. I asked for the Lord's presence to flood her and show her that she was not alone.

I could feel the "rush" of Him as He came to her, full of love and compassion. What happened was an instantaneous response to a daughter who needed a touch from Him. Both of us were overwhelmed. We have such a good and gracious God! When our hearts are desperate, He does not drag His feet.

I was reminded of this point one morning when I was driving to school. I had all kinds of things on my mind, mostly about my lessons and plans for the day. Suddenly, my mind flitted to Jesus. I received just a glimpse of His face in my mind. Instantly, His presence filled my car. I began to weep with the wonder of the experience. By the time I was in the parking lot, I was sobbing. He is so ready to meet with us, to commune with us. I felt so loved!

I shared this story with a woman at the altar and told her that God was so close to her that with just a glimpse in His direction, He would be there to comfort her. Sometimes, I think we feel like we need to beg, plead, or make some grandiose gesture to gain God's ear.

Just the contrary. He sees the tiniest glimpse of our eye. He hears the softest of cries, the quietest sighs. His ear is attuned to us because He loves us so much.

Later, the woman shared with me that what I said helped her so much to have that physical reminder—to look out the corner of her eye and catch a glimpse and know He was there. I hope this encourages anyone who feels all alone.

God is our refuge and strength,
a very present help in trouble.
PSALM 46:1

In the multitudes of my anxieties within me,
Your comforts delight my soul.
PSALM 94:19

51
Rejoice in the Lord

Rejoice in the Lord! Throw back your head and sing His praises into the heavens! Dance before Him with abandon. He is worthy, worthy, worthy! Our God is a good God. There is none like Him in all the heavens or on the earth. How privileged we are to call Him "Daddy God"! We are His chosen ones, His favorite ones. We are the apple of His eye. Let us live this day and every day in these wondrous truths. No grumbling, no fear, no worry. Look to Him. Settle yourself in His presence with joy and expectancy.

Our God reigns! Hallelujah!

Be glad in the Lord and rejoice, you righteous;
And shout for joy, all you upright in heart!
Psalm 32:11

Sing to God, sing praises to His name;
Extol Him who rides on the clouds,
By His name YAH,
And rejoice before Him.
Psalm 68:4

52
Preach Jesus

"Preach Jesus. Use words if necessary."

No one is sure who issued that challenge, but how do we share the Gospel without using words? Most of us want to talk, talk, talk to get our point across, but how did Jesus live? What example did He set? What was His emphasis?

If I could choose one word to describe Jesus, it would be *love*. Unconditional, unwavering love. His love overlooked where people came from, what they looked or smelled like, how they made their living, or how influential they were in their community. He looked straight into their hearts and loved them from the inside out.

So, how should we live our lives in order to "preach Jesus"? We start by demonstrating love.

1 Corinthians 13 tells us that love is patient and kind, not envious, puffed up, rude, or easily provoked. Love rejoices in truth, but not sin. Love bears all things, believes all things, and endures all things.

This is the essence of who Jesus is. This is how we need to live. We need to pursue love and show love. That isn't easy for us, but we can do all things through Christ. His grace is always sufficient, right?

And now abide faith, hope, love, these three;
but the greatest of these is love.
1 Corinthians 13:13

And this commandment we have from Him:
that he who loves God must love his brother also.
1 John 4:21

53
True Peace

This world doesn't know true peace. They have a fleeting glance as they are pulled and pushed by the spirit of this world. They are in a race for money, influence, goods, and time, all just a little out of their reach. Their insides are churning, their blood pressure is soaring, and their life is like being on a treadmill, going nowhere. I am sad to see My people falling into the same trap. I want to remind you that on the cross, I made peace available to you. It is there for the taking, but your eyes and thoughts need to be settled upon Me. You need to turn everything over to Me daily, and trust Me. I am your peace.

And the peace of God, which surpasses all understanding, will guard your hearts and minds through Christ Jesus.
PHILIPPIANS 4:7

And let the peace of God rule in your hearts to which also you were called in one body; and be thankful.
COLOSSIANS 3:15

For He Himself is our peace . . .
EPHESIANS 2:14A

*"The Lord bless you and keep you;
The Lord make His face shine upon you,
And be gracious to you;
The Lord lift up His countenance upon you,
And give you peace."*
NUMBERS 6:24-26

54
Overpowering Love

My love can overpower you. Just let it come. Let every crevice, every pocket of doubt, every regret be filled with My love. Drink it in; wallow in it. Walk in it, and reach out to others in it. Remember: I am love. My very essence flows through you. I am using you on earth. Every smile, every touch, and every kind word is an expression of My love. Be the carrier of My love today.

> *Therefore be imitators of God as dear children. And walk in love, as Christ also has loved us and given Himself for us, an offering and a sacrifice to God for a sweet-smelling aroma.*
> **Ephesians 5:1-2**

> *Therefore, as the elect of God, holy and beloved, put on tender mercies, kindness, humility, meekness, longsuffering; bearing with one another and forgiving one another; if anyone has a complaint against another; even as Christ forgave you, so you also must do. But above all these things put on love, which is the bond of perfection.*
> **Colossians 3:12-14**

55
My Yoke Is Light

Let My yoke be light. Let yourself be carried by Me. It should not be a hard task, a taxing of the spirit and mind. There is an ease in walking with Me. When you strive in your relationship with Me, it becomes "of the flesh" and not of the Spirit. There is rest in Me, not work. I "lifted" you up out of the miry clay and set you on the rock, not intending for you to "bury" yourself under worries and fears. Let your spirit soar as you commune with Me! It should not be a burden, but a joy. That is My desire for you.

> *He also brought me up out of a horrible pit,*
> *Out of the miry clay,*
> *And set my feet upon a rock,*
> *And established my steps.*
> *He has put a new song in my mouth—*
> *Praise to our God;*
> *Many will see it and fear,*
> *And will trust in the Lord.*
>
> **Psalm 40:2-3**

> *"Come to Me, all you who labor and are heavy laden, and I will give you rest. Take My yoke upon you and learn from Me, for I am gentle and lowly in heart, and you will find rest for your souls. For My yoke is easy and My burden is light."*
>
> **Matthew 11:28-30**

I needed to hear this Word from the Lord. Without thinking about it, I find myself striving spiritually, wanting to do everything on my own in my desire to please Him.

It doesn't have to be that way. In fact, it's good to know that He really wants us to just keep our eyes on Him and let Him to do His work in us.

A popular saying goes like this: "Let go, and let God." I think that's good advice to follow—for you and for me.

56
He Never Changes

Circumstances change. I do not. Weather changes. I do not. Feelings change. Relationships change. I remain the same. I am your rock, your strong tower. I am immovable. I am your constant. When you feel rattled or shaken, cling to Me. When things seem out of control, I am your stabilizer. When a little child is upset, they seek out their mother or father. They want to crawl up on a parent's lap and be held. It is the same for you. Come to Me. My arms are open wide, and My lap is always available for you. Come.

> *The Lord is my rock, and my fortress and my deliverer;*
> *The God of my strength, in whom I will trust;*
> *My shield and the horn of my salvation,*
> *My stronghold and my refuge.*
> **2 Samuel 22:2-3a**

> *When my heart is overwhelmed;*
> *Lead me to the rock that is higher than I.*
> **Psalm 61:2b**

I am thankful that our God is a rock, a sure foundation. The things of this world are unreliable and ever-changing, but we can stand firm in Him.

57
My Word

My Word is My gift to you. For in My Word you will find wisdom, strength, direction, and purpose. By My Word, you can change your world. Speaking My Word can alter the atmosphere around you. Power is found in My Word—to heal the sick, to raise up and bring down those in authority, to bring increase to every area of your life.

Pray My Word. It pleases Me to hear My Word spoken back to Me in faith. I am bound to My Word. Do not regard it lightly. It is your weapon against the enemy. It is to be savored and cherished.

As I received this Word, I thought of Psalm 119, which is all about God's Word and its benefits. Here are a few of my favorite verses from that psalm:

Open my eyes, that I may see
Wondrous things from Your law.
PSALM 119:18

Forever, O Lord,
Your word is settled in heaven.
PSALM 119:89

How sweet are Your words to my taste,
Sweeter than honey to my mouth!
PSALM 119:103

Psalm 119 is incredibly encouraging to read, so try to read this psalm—the longest psalm and longest chapter in the Bible—from beginning to end. When you spend that much time in God's Word, you can be strengthened and encouraged.

58
He Is Love

Recently, thoughts swirling around in my head and heart were centered on how much I love Jesus. I *so* love the Lord! I am constantly falling more and more in love with Him.

When I think I truly know Him, like an onion, He peels away another layer of Himself, and I fall even more helplessly into His deep love. Think about it: Divine revelation! How amazing He is! He is the Lover of my soul. His love is constant—no ups and downs on His end. He makes me feel like a love-struck teenager. I just want to hang around in His presence.

No one loves us like He does because His love is unconditional. His love is never fickle. He gave His life on the Cross because of His great love for us. He pours love into us constantly. Every time I think I'm so full of His love, He expands my heart so that I can receive more.

I'll say it again: He is love!

In this the love of God was manifested toward us, that God has sent His only begotten Son into the world, that we might live through Him.
1 John 4:9

We love Him because He first loved us.
1 John 4:19

59
Roots

I love spring! The warm temperatures lift my spirit and even put a little "spring" in my step. With longer days and warmer sunshine, my mind becomes filled with thoughts of new life stirring under the ground, waiting to come forth. Grass, flowers, shrubs, budding trees—I love springtime.

That brings me to the topic of roots because the roots of plants, trees, and shrubs need nourishment to grow and produce fruit. Roots also keep trees and vegetation anchored to the ground.

In a similar fashion, we need our spiritual roots to grow. The deeper our roots grow, the stronger we become in the Lord and the more likely others will see fruit in our lives. Our roots anchor us, enabling us to weather life's storms.

How do our roots grow stronger and deeper? By spending time with the Lord, by being in His Word, and by resting in His presence.

I love these verses about being "planted" in Him:

> *But I am like a green olive tree in the house of God;*
> *I trust in the mercy of God forever and forever.*
> **Psalm 52:8**

> *As you therefore have received Christ Jesus the Lord,*
> *so walk in Him, rooted and built up in Him and*
> *established in the faith, as you have been taught,*
> *abounding in it with thanksgiving.*
> **Colossians 2:6-7**

> *For this reason I bow my knees to the Father of our Lord Jesus Christ . . .*
> *that Christ may dwell in your hearts through faith; that you, being rooted*
> *and grounded in love, may be able to comprehend with all the saints what is*
> *the width, and length and depth and height—to know the love of Christ which*
> *passes knowledge; that you may be filled with all the fullness of God.*
> **Ephesians 3:14, 17-19**

60
Sing

It can be difficult to walk worthy of our calling on days when our best-laid plans go awry and emotions run high. What about those "worst days"? What can you do to hold it together?

One thing you can do is sing. Yes, you read correctly. Even if you can't carry a tune in a bucket, you can play your favorite worship tunes and hum along. Singing changes your focus, soothes your heart, and stimulates your faith.

The enemy would love your days to be filled with discord, tension, confusion, and discouragement. Singing can be used as a weapon against the adversary.

Joyful singing in the middle of conflict confounds the enemy. In 2 Chronicles 20, Jehoshaphat, the king of Judah, was about to lead his army against the enemy, who vastly outnumbered them. He called his people together, and they praised the Lord with voices high and loud (vs. 19). He appointed people to sing to the Lord, and they were sent out *before* the army. As they sang praises, the Lord set ambushes against the enemy, and they were defeated. Judah's army didn't even have to fight. I'd say that was pretty amazing!

When I first walked into my classroom each morning, I liked to play Christian music. (This was when I taught in a Christian school.) Those wonderful songs of praise invaded the atmosphere and prepared my heart for the day.

I'm not saying my days of teaching youngsters went perfectly, but I'd hate to think of how much worse my school day could have been if I hadn't started my mornings that way. When your focus is set on Him, He is pleased and I believe that He, in turn, sings over us. I want His song in my heart and on my lips.

Behold, God is my salvation,
I will trust and not be afraid;
For YAH, the Lord, is my strength and song;
He also has become my salvation.
ISAIAH 12:2

Make a joyful shout to the Lord, all you lands!
Serve the Lord with gladness;
Come before His presence with singing.
PSALM 100:1-2

You are a hiding place;
You shall preserve me from trouble;
You shall surround me with songs of deliverance.
PSALM 32:

61
Our Words

When we talk about the tongue, you might think of the verses in the Book of James that admonish us to control the fleshy organ used to articulate speech.

I want to take an opposite tack: I want to concentrate on how you can use your tongue and the words you say in a positive way. I'm sure you're just like me in that we could probably share a time when someone said something to us that lifted our spirits and made us feel good about ourselves.

Words can encourage, comfort, enlighten, and inspire us, so much so that I can remember words that were spoken to me over forty years ago. What was said to me back then was kind and made me look at myself differently.

Because words are so powerful, we should look for opportunities to speak into people's lives, to open their eyes to new possibilities, and give them hope and increase their faith.

Words can also be weapons for good. For instance, we can speak truth and defeat the lies of the enemy. We can speak Scripture over someone, which may result in a spiritual breakthrough. We can "call out" abilities and spiritual giftings. We can "build up" when the enemy is trying to "tear down."

Give your tongue to the Lord, and let Him use it for His purposes.

A word fitly spoken is like apples of gold
In settings of silver.
Like an earring of gold and an ornament of fine gold
Is a wise rebuker to an obedient ear.
PROVERBS 25:11-12

By long forbearance a ruler is persuaded,
And a gentle tongue breaks a bone.
PROVERBS 25:15

Let the words of my mouth and the meditation of my heart
Be acceptable in Your sight,
O Lord, my strength and my Redeemer.
PSALM 19:14

62
My Peace

There is no peace like My peace. People try to create a peaceful environment. They may meditate, trying to work up a peace within themselves. My peace is not dependent upon the environment. It is not affected by circumstances or other people. My peace cannot be reproduced or created. Peace is My gift to those who seek Me, those who trust Me.

The world becomes more and more restless and chaotic. People are searching for peace in many ways, but they will never find it, apart from Me. My people who are called by My name receive freely from Me. I gladly pour out My peace upon them. In turn, they can affect the world around them as they carry it into their homes, neighborhoods, and workplaces.

Be a carrier of peace, not turmoil or worry. Keep your eyes on Me and your heart tuned to Mine. You will live a peace-filled life.

Peace I leave with you, My peace
I give to you; not as the world gives do
I give to you. Let not your heart be
troubled, neither let it be afraid.
JOHN 14:27

Be anxious for nothing, but in everything by prayer
and supplication, with thanksgiving, let your requests
be made known to God; and the peace of God,
which passes all understanding, will guard your
hearts and minds through Christ Jesus.
PHILIPPIANS 4:6-7

63
Name Above All Names

Some people are known for being "name-droppers," implying that they have a relationship with a well-known person and are even on a first-name basis with that person. They drop names to make themselves feel important, to impress others, and increase their prestige.

Well, there's a "name above all names" to drop, and it's the name of Jesus. We don't need to use His name to impress anyone. Instead, when we say Jesus' name, we can talk about how circumstances change, attitudes shift, bodies are healed, hearts are softened, and minds are calmed. We can say His name because we put our trust in Him. He is the source for every one of our needs.

The Bible says the name of Jesus is like ointment poured forth. Ointment is used to sooth, restore, heal, or make fragrant. His name can accomplish the same results in your life. Speak "Jesus" over your circumstances. Let's tell others about Him. Live your life in a way that brings honor to His name and spreads His fragrance wherever you go.

> *Because of the fragrance of your good ointments,*
> *Your name is ointment poured forth.*
> **Song of Solomon 1:3a**

> *Therefore God also has highly exalted Him and given Him the name which is above every name.*
> **Philippians 2:9**

> *"They will call upon My name,*
> *And I will answer them.*
> *I will say, 'This is My people';*
> *And each one will say, 'The Lord is my God.' "*
> **Zechariah 13:9**

64
A Mountain

If there is a mountain in front of you, you can climb it in My strength. If there is a problem that seems unsolvable, My wisdom is yours. If you can't focus or concentrate, you have My peace and the mind of Christ. If you suffer pain or illness, I am the Great Healer and Comforter. I am the source for your every need. Pull on Me. Grab hold of what has already been provided for you. I offer it in love.

I think all of us have had a "mountain" in our life, something that seemed insurmountable.

This Word from the Lord renews my faith. We can do anything with His help. I am so glad that we have a "where the tire meets the road" kind of God. Nothing is too difficult for Him. Nothing is too small. He doesn't get in a tizzy over anything! He is the faithful one, always watching over us, and waiting for us to call on Him.

> *But let all those rejoice who put their trust in You;*
> *Let them ever shout for joy, because You defend them;*
> *Let those also who love Your name*
> *Be joyful in You.*
> *For You, O Lord, will bless the righteous;*
> *With favor You will surround him as with a shield.*
> **Psalm 5:11-12**

65
Moments

Moments spent with Me are well-spent moments. I who have created the world can surely work miracles or minister to you in just a moment. Grab as many moments as you can in a day to let your mind rest on Me. Consider Me. Love Me. Listen to Me. Let Me be your oasis of refreshment. I am always available. I am a moment-by-moment God.

If you're like me, there never seems to be enough time in a day, which is why this Word is an encouragement to me. What the Lord is saying is a gentle reminder of what we already know. He is an available God. He can change our attitude or our circumstances in a moment.

What a great God we have! The more moments we spend with Him, the more we become like Him. That is my heart's cry!

> *. . . so that times of refreshing may come from the presence of the Lord.*
> ACTS 3:19B

> *Rest in the Lord, and wait patiently for Him.*
> PSALM 37:7A

> *You will keep him in perfect peace,*
> *Whose mind is stayed on You,*
> *Because he trusts in You.*
> ISAIAH 26:3

66
Bless the Lord Your God

In the ninth chapter of Nehemiah, the Israelites had rebuilt the wall around Jerusalem and were having a sacred assembly. They read from the Book of the Law for one-fourth of the day and worshipped another fourth of the day.

Then the leaders of the Israelites stood up and began to speak out the attributes of God and all the things He had done for His people, starting with the creation of the world, the choosing of their leader, Abraham, the dividing of the Red Sea to provide escape from Egypt, and the giving of the Ten Commandments. The clear message: throughout the past, God had cared for them and provided for them. The pronouncements were a vivid reminder that He was gracious to them, even when they were fickle and disobedient.

After reading this section from Nehemiah, I began praising God and telling Him how much I loved Him. He is such a good God! And then God responded to me with this Word:

Whatever I did for the Israelites, I will do for you: blessings, provisions, mercy, grace, and favor. You are My people, My beloved, My chosen ones. Don't worry. Don't fret. Don't give in to fear. Read and re-read My Word, and strengthen yourself in the inner man. Feed your spirit daily, and let it build your faith. Let it reveal to you the times and seasons, and let it reveal My ways, so that you may find comfort.

"Stand up and bless the Lord your God
Forever and ever!

"Blessed be Your glorious name,
Which is exalted above all blessing and praise!
You alone are the Lord;
You have made heaven,
The heaven of heavens, with all their host,
The earth and everything on it,
The seas and all that is in them,
And You preserve them all
The host of heaven worships you."

Nehemiah 9:5b-6

67
Live in the Now

Do not be consumed by what tomorrow brings or what the past holds. Live today in the "now." Be present in My presence. It makes all the difference.

What a good reminder for me! How about you? Are you living in a "whirlwind"? What if you concentrated on His presence in the midst of a maelstrom? What do you think the difference would be?

This is what Lord God says:

> "Because he has set his love upon Me, therefore I will deliver him;
> I will set him on high, because he has known My name.
> He shall call upon Me, and I will answer him.
> I will be with him in trouble;
> I will deliver him and honor him.
> With long life I will satisfy him,
> And show My salvation.
> **Psalm 91:14-16**

Focus on these words and phrases from this Scripture:

Deliverance . . . set on high . . . helped in trouble . . . honor . . . a long life . . . His salvation . . . not to mention His great love, which is always with us.

Do these make the difference? I would say, "Yes and amen, our Emmanuel!" Experience His presence today and be blessed!

68
Look Beyond

For a whole day, this phrase kept coming to my mind: *Look beyond.* I finally realized that God was telling me something. As sensual beings, we use our senses to understand our world. We need to see, hear, and feel in order to believe. We often use the "show me" approach in our daily lives.

When making a decision, we want to see what's behind "Door Number 1" before we choose. Life doesn't always allow us that luxury, however. God wants us to know that *He* is behind every door. He wants us to trust *Him* to guide us as we make those decisions. Don't be concerned with the "unknown," but concentrate on the "known," which is this: God is a wise, faithful, and loving God.

When I read *The Veil* by Blake K. Healy, who talks about the spiritual realm being a real place, the following quote really struck me: "You may not be aware of it, but you exist in the spiritual realm just as much as you exist in the physical. You are one hundred percent there and one hundred percent here."

Reading those words made me so excited! This is why we can affect the atmosphere around us in the physical, and the more we are aware of the spiritual, the more our faith and trust grows. We become bolder as we live out our faith in the physical.

As we learn to "look beyond," we truly learn to walk in His power. I want that so much!

> *For since the beginning of the world*
> *Men have not heard nor perceived by the ear,*
> *Nor has the eye seen any God besides You,*
> *Who acts for the one who waits for Him.*
> **Isaiah 64:4**

> *But God has revealed them to us through His Spirit.*
> *For the Spirit searches all things, yes, the deep things of God.*
> *Now we have received, not the spirit of the world,*
> *but the Spirit who is from God, that we might know*
> *the things that have been freely given to us by God.*
> **1 Corinthians 2:10, 12**

I don't want to miss one thing that He has for me!

69
Loads of Benefits

> *Blessed be the Lord,*
> *Who daily loads us with benefits,*
> *The God of our salvation!*
> **Psalm 68:19**

This Bible verse is a simple statement of a wondrous truth. God is good, and we are the beneficiaries of that goodness. He is a generous God!

Consider the benefits we have:

- freedom from sin
- freedom from our old selves
- love
- joy (regardless of our circumstances)
- faith (regardless of our circumstances)
- peace (yup, you guessed it—regardless of our circumstances)
- wisdom
- love
- grace
- direction
- blessings
- love
- food, clothing, and shelter
- families
- friends
- the body of believers
- and more love

This list is only scratching the surface because we serve an awesome God! He is constant in His love for us. These benefits aren't just on our good days but even when we fall short. He doesn't easily flip the switch off, yank the chain, or pull the plug from the source.

Instead, He is always there, always available for us. There is no one else in heaven or on earth like Him, and He calls us His own! I am forever grateful.

70
Live, Move, and Be

*I beseech you therefore, brethren, by the mercies of God,
that you present your bodies a living sacrifice,
holy, acceptable to God, which is your reasonable service.*
ROMANS 12:1

When you offer your body as a living sacrifice, it involves everything about you—your thoughts, your words, your actions. What do these things show about you? Your thoughts, words, and actions should reflect Me. You have the power to build up or tear down, to bless or to curse. What will it be?

Positive begets positive, negative begets negative. Live in the positive. Choose life. The negative chooses sin and death. You need to purposely choose to live, move, and have your being in Me. Then you will be a blessing to others and bring joy to Me.

For in Him we live and move and have our being . . .
ACTS 17:28A

Think of how you should interact with others: What attitude are you displaying? What words are you using? What are your actions?

Give yourself over to God afresh and ask Him to use you as a blessing to others. What a privilege!

71
Lie Back

Lie back against Me. Breathe Me in. Breathe fear and worry out. Draw your strength from My presence. Lay it all at My feet and trust Me. *I am your God.*

One day, fierce storms hit my hometown of Omaha, Nebraska. While my daughter was driving home in the midst of these storms, a tree fell on her van. Fortunately, she was fine, but when I saw the pictures of her destroyed van, I experienced shock from thinking about what the outcome could have been.

In the same week, I prayed for dear friends who had loved ones suffering from cancer. That often-fatal illness brings fear and a feeling of helplessness to millions seeking treatment each day.

Trials like these can change everything in a matter of seconds. Burdensome troubles make us realize that we are not in charge. Life intervenes when we least expect it. We can experience fear, worry, and doubt in a New York minute.

The Lord's Word to us today shows me that He understands what we are feeling. He wants us to turn everything over to Him. We have to remember that *He* is in charge. He is the Lord God Almighty, ruler of heaven and earth, and He chooses to draw us under His wings, even as we walk through hard times.

Remember: He will carry you in His strong arms because He is a good God!

> *Even to your old age, I am He,*
> *And even to gray hairs I will carry you!*
> *I have made, and I will bear;*
> *Even I will carry, and will deliver you.*
> **Isaiah 46:4**

> *How precious is Your lovingkindness, O God!*
> *Therefore the children of men put their trust*
> *under the shadow of Your wings.*
> **Psalm 36:7**

72
Cast Away

"Cast away from you all the transgressions which you have committed, and get yourselves a new heart and a new spirit. For why should you die, O house of Israel? For I have no pleasure in the death of one who dies," says the Lord God. "Therefore turn and live!"

Ezekiel 18:31-32

The Lord, speaking to the house of Israel, was reminding them that all souls are His, and the ones who keep their trust in Him and are just in their ways will surely live. Those who ignore God's laws and are involved in sin, however, shall die.

We are under a new covenant, but the basic truth is when we trust God and live for Him, our lives will be blessed. When dabbling in sin and doing things that are in opposition to Him, we die spiritually. I choose life in every facet of its meaning.

Are you clinging to sinful actions or attitudes that need to be changed? Are you single-minded when it comes to the Lord, or have you become influenced by our world? Are you in the Word daily, or have you let that slide?

I know we all lead busy lives, and sometimes before we know it, we have been pulled away and are no longer hitting the mark. As I examine my own life, I am thankful that God is faithful to point out what I need to change and lovingly helps me get back on track.

Let Him do that for you, too.

73
Carry One Another

Carry one another. Share the burdens around you. I never intended for you to live like an island, apart from everything and everyone. The body of Christ must infiltrate lives and express love, for I am love. Minister to one another and to the lost. Pray for one another, and pray for the lost. Be My hand extended. There is coming a day when needs will be great, and fear will be all around you. Build relationships through love now, so you can be a bright light in that darkness.

God is love. His Word says that we will be known by our love for one another. Let's demonstrate to the world the love of the Father.

*Blessed be the God and Father of our Lord Jesus Christ,
the Father of mercies and God of all comfort, who comforts us
in all our tribulation, that we may be able to comfort those
who are in any trouble, with the comfort with which
we ourselves are comforted by God.*
2 CORINTHIANS 1:3-4

74
Bible Stories

One day, I was reading in the Gospel of Matthew. It was the story about Peter walking on water to get to Jesus. As I read through Chapter 14, the Lord laid this on my heart:

The world looks at the Bible as a collection of interesting stories and great poetry. They do not take it as truth but are filled with skepticism. The accounts in My Word are true, and each one was included to reveal who I am. I don't ask My people today to walk on the water, but the story indicates that if you keep your eyes on Me, you will get through difficult circumstances. You will experience My peace. Sometimes getting through a difficult day seems like "walking on water." But when your eyes are set on Me, you can do anything.

The parting of the Red Sea has been made into a joke by some. It is an account of My people being set free and demonstrates My power and the great love I have for My people. It shows that I can make a way when it seems impossible. I am a God of the impossible. Apply that to your finances, your relationships, and your life-changing decisions.

The more you are in My Word, the more you learn about Me. The more you know about Me, the more your faith grows. I fed thousands with five loaves and two fish. Surely, I can provide for you. I know your every need. I want you to trust Me with each one. When you look to Me in faith, it causes Me to move on your behalf. My Word is My message of love to you.

Thank you, Lord, for your Word. Thank you that it increases our knowledge of You and Your ways. Thank you that it builds our faith, and shows us how to live our lives for You.

Blessed are the undefiled in the way,
Who walk in the law of the Lord!
Blessed are those who keep His testimonies,
Who seek Him with the whole heart!
PSALM 119:1-2

75
Change

Change is a part of everyone's life. Change can bring fear. Change can bring joy. Change can take you by surprise, or it can be something you know will happen even though it's a long way off.

For me, change was retirement. I knew it was coming, but it still took me by surprise, even after thirty-seven years of teaching.

So what is the best way to handle change? Sometimes there's nothing you can do to prevent changes happening in your life. You just have to embrace a new direction as another step with God, another challenge that can strengthen your walk with Him and create a testimony of His unfailing grace.

As I was contemplating these thoughts, I read these favorite verses of mine. I believe they are encouraging for anyone who is going through a change or is facing an "unknown" in their lives:

> *How precious is your lovingkindness, O God!*
> *Therefore the children of men put their trust under the shadow of Your wings.*
> *They are abundantly satisfied with the fullness of Your house.*
> *And you give them drink from the river of Your pleasures.*
> *For with You is the fountain of life;*
> *In Your light we see light.*
> **PSALM 36:7-9**

> *Trust in the Lord, and do good;*
> *Dwell in the land, and feed on His faithfulness.*
> *Delight yourself also in the Lord,*
> *And He shall give you the desires of your heart.*
>
> *Commit your way to the Lord,*
> *Trust also in Him,*
> *And He shall bring it to pass.*
> **PSALM 37:3-5**

God is kind toward us. He protects us. He abundantly satisfies us. He is faithful. He gives us the desires of our heart, and when we trust Him, He takes us through our walk, whatever that may be.

What a gracious God! The more we know Him, the more He quells our fears with His very presence. Thank you, Lord!

76
Listen

*L*isten up!

When we hear those words, we expect an announcement, important information, or directions. Our ears perk up in anticipation.

That's how we need to listen when the Lord speaks. In 1 Samuel 3, the Lord speaks to Samuel, a boy who ministers to the Lord under Eli. He speaks to him several times, and each time He calls, Samuel says, "Speak, Lord, for your servant hears."

Scripture says that a Word from the Lord was very rare in those days; there was no widespread revelation. Even so, the Lord spoke to a mere boy, Samuel, and told him a prophetic Word concerning his mentor, Eli. Why did God choose him? I think it was because God knew that Samuel would listen.

God still speaks today, and He wants His people to listen. One way He speaks to us is through His written Word. Throughout the pages of the Bible, we learn the character of God and how He interacts with His people, as well as how we can live a life which pleases Him. With the help of Holy Spirit, the Word can be opened up to us in a revelatory way, revealing more than what meets the eye.

The Lord also speaks to our minds and our hearts. When we are tuned into Him, we can hear a still small voice like Elijah did in 1 Kings 19:12.

I want to always be tuned into His frequency so that I do not miss a single word that He has for me, and I urge you to feel the same way.

> *While he [Peter] was still speaking, behold a bright cloud overshadowed them; and suddenly a voice came out of the cloud, saying, "This is My beloved Son, in whom I am well pleased. Hear Him!"*
> **MATTHEW 17:5**

> *Like an earring of gold and an ornament of fine gold Is a wise rebuker to an obedient ear.*
> **PROVERBS 25:12**

> *Behold, I stand at the door and knock. If anyone hears My voice and opens the door, I will come in to him and dine with him, and he with Me.*
> **REVELATION 3:20**

77
Jesus Is . . .

While having my time in God's Word one day, I was drawn to the verses that tell who Jesus is to us. He is our . . .

- Savior
- horn of salvation
- shepherd
- shield
- strong tower
- refuge
- shelter
- strength
- peace
- fortress
- deliverer
- husband
- lover of our soul
- stronghold
- lifter of our head
- counselor
- King of Kings
- Lord of Lords

You probably have a favorite descriptor, one that carried you through a difficult circumstance or brought you to a spiritual pinnacle. I love them all and am overwhelmed by the Lord. I'm grateful that He calls me *His* child.

Among the gods there is none like You, O Lord;
Nor are there any works like Your works.
All nations whom You have made
Shall come and worship before You, O Lord,
And shall glorify Your name.
For You are great, and do wondrous things;
You alone are God.
PSALM 86:8-10

78
Influence Our Culture

King Nebuchadnezzar of Babylon had a golden statue created and ordered that everyone should bow down to it. Of course, most people bowed down to avoid any retribution, but Daniel and his friends refused to prostrate themselves. They said they would worship only the one true God.

One time I heard a speaker talk about how God-fearing people like Daniel changed the culture around them. This statement stuck with me:

They stood when others bowed, and they bowed when others stood.

How do we influence our culture? That's a great and important question to ask since many feel we are living in a post-Christian world.

Are you a "doer" of the Word? Do you stay in close communication with God? Do you stand up for your beliefs, or do you "pick and choose" from the Bible what you are going to believe—and then live a life that allows you to "fit in" with the rest of the world? Finally, do you bow to idols, or do you worship the one true God in spirit and in truth?

Back in Nebuchadnezzar's time, it was the law to bow down to the golden statue. When laws are passed today that go against the Word of God, does it change how you should live? Does it make it right to sin because it's "legal" in the eyes of today's society?

Daniel's actions make me even more determined to not bow down to the world for the sake of the gospel.

> ***But he who looks into the perfect law of liberty and continues in it, and is not a forgetful hearer but a doer of the work, this one will be blessed in what he does.***
> **JAMES 1:25**

79
Jehovah Jireh

I am Jehovah Jireh, the one who provides. Whatever your need, I am your source. Do not limit Me or put Me in a box. Don't expect My provision in only *some* areas, but in *all* areas—physical, financial, spiritual, emotional, and relational.

Are you lacking understanding? Then I am your source of revelation. Difficulty making a decision? I am your wisdom. Wonder how you can pay your bills? Then look to Me.

Trust Me in the small things and the big. Nothing is too inconsequential. If you need a parking spot quickly because you are in a time crunch, I can provide. If you are tired and can't think of what to make for dinner, I can help you be creative because I am the Creator.

I am a practical God. I want you to depend on Me completely. Doing so is not a sign of weakness. Rather, it is a sign of faith in the One who loves you most.

Thank you, Lord, for being our provider in all aspects of our life.

And my God shall supply all your need
according to His riches in glory by Christ Jesus.
Philippians 4:19

But Jesus looked at them and said to them,
"With men this is impossible,
but with God all things are possible."
Matthew 19:26

You will keep him in perfect peace,
Whose mind is stayed on You,
Because he trusts in You.
Trust in the Lord forever,
For in YAH, the Lord, is everlasting strength.
Isaiah 26:3-4

80
I Am Your God

I *am* your God. There is no shadow of turning with Me. I am the same yesterday, today, and forever. I am the God of Abraham, Isaac, and Jacob, and I am *your* God. You are My chosen one, My royal priesthood. You are seated with Me in the heavenlies. In My name, you are given all authority. How then do you live? You abide in Me. You trust in Me. You walk in integrity and strength, knowing that I *am* your God.

We need to see ourselves as God sees us. We are the ones He chose. We need to walk out our lives, knowing not just who we are, but *whose* we are.

> *. . . that you may walk worthy of the Lord,*
> *fully pleasing Him, being fruitful in every good work*
> *and increasing in the knowledge of God; strengthened*
> *with all might, according to His glorious power, for all*
> *patience and longsuffering with joy; giving thanks to*
> *the Father who has qualified us to be partakers*
> *of the inheritance of the saints in the light.*
> **COLOSSIANS 1:10-12**

81
His Waves

I was daydreaming about what it would be like to sit by a lake and watch the water come in over the pebbles and sand on the shore. How lovely and relaxing. While I was thinking on this, God shared this Word:

>See the water at its edges, as it flows up upon the sand? It moves constantly, sometimes in big, powerful waves, and at other times, in gentle lapping. So it is with Me. I am always moving. Sometimes in big waves, sometimes in quiet, small ripples. Just know I am always there.
>
>I am always working in your life. I am wearing down. I am building up. I am altering. I am making ready. Never doubt, but in faith, welcome My waves.

Does it ever seem to you like you are being swept along by something beyond your control? Even though you don't know what's around the next corner, you just keep hanging on.

As His children, we can know that He is in charge, and even when times or circumstances are not pleasant, we have to trust that He always has our best interests in mind. He is our loving Abba, our Daddy God. He sees us from the beginning to the end, so we want to hold onto Him and let Him do His work. We want to welcome His waves.

> *As for God, His way is perfect;*
> *The Word of the Lord is proven;*
> *He is a shield to all who trust in Him.*
>
> *For who is God, except the Lord?*
> *And who is a rock, except our God?*
> *It is God who arms me with strength,*
> *And makes my way perfect.*
> **Psalm 18:30-32**

> *Wait on the Lord;*
> *Be of good courage,*
> *And He will strengthen your heart;*
> *Wait, I say, on the Lord!*
> **Psalm 27:14**

82
Do Not Fear

"Have I not commanded you? Be strong and of good courage; do not be afraid, nor be dismayed, for the Lord your God is with you wherever you go."
Joshua 1:9

There is much fear in the world today. Massive earthquakes, enormous forest fires, tremendous hurricanes, unexpected floods, horrific terrorist attacks, and mass shootings.

Some shootings in the news resulted in people dying because they were Christians. My first thought was that this will occur more often. The Bible warns us that this will happen, but the Church is now experiencing fear when we should be fixing our eyes on Jesus, the one who suffered a violent death so that we could overcome this world.

Fear is not from God. He is our peace, our strength, and our Rock. These following Scriptures should encourage us no matter what is causing our fear:

For God has not given us a spirit of fear,
but of power and of love and of a sound mind.
2 Timothy 1:7

The Lord is my light and my salvation;
Whom shall I fear?
The Lord is the strength of my life;
Of whom shall I be afraid?
Psalm 27:1

For by You I can run against a troop,
By my God I can leap over a wall.
As for God, His way is perfect;
The word of the Lord is proven;
He is a shield to all who trust in Him.
Psalm 18:29-30

Now I know that the Lord saves His anointed;
He will answer him from His holy heaven
With the saving strength of His right hand.
Psalm 20:6

Now I'd like you to read Psalm 91 in its entirety.

If you are one who is experiencing fear, I pray that the peace of God will settle upon you as you read these Scriptures.

83
I Have a God

I have a God who always loves me—always!

I have a God who is not angry with me.

I have a God who is always for me, never against me.

I have a God who understands me more than I understand myself.

I have a God who opens doors and closes others.

I have a God who is always faithful, never fickle.

I have a God who sees me as no one else sees me because He sees my future self.

I have a God who can send legions of angels to surround me.

I have a God who parts traffic, finds parking spots, and leads me to great sales. He is interested in every aspect of my life.

I could go on and on. He is an amazing God!

I will bless the Lord at all times;
His praise shall continually be in my mouth.
My soul shall make its boast in the Lord;
The humble shall hear of it and be glad.
Oh magnify the Lord with me,
And let us exalt His name together.
Psalm 34:1-3

84
A Cheerful Heart

A cheerful heart is a blessing to all those around you and is even an encouragement to your own spirit. Negative begets negative; positive begets positive. Which do you represent? What emanates from your actions, your words, your countenance? When you enter a room do people cringe, or do they want to smile? You are My chosen ones, and you represent Me. Let people see the joy of the Lord in you. Be the salt that makes them thirsty for Me.

This Word drives me to repentance. We all have days when nothing seems to go right. Maybe people irritate us or are rude to us. Our family members might have disappointed us—or maybe we disappointed them. It really doesn't matter what the situation is, but we need to ask ourselves, "Am I pleasing God? Am I giving a good witness?"

I'm thankful that the Lord is a gracious, loving God who always gives us second chances. I choose to honor Him in my daily life, no matter what the circumstances.

A merry heart does good, like medicine.
Proverbs 17:22a

A soft answer turns away wrath,
But a harsh word stirs up anger.
Proverbs 15:1

A merry heart makes a cheerful countenance.
Proverbs 15:13a

When a man's ways please the Lord,
He makes even his enemies to be at peace with him.
Proverbs 16:7

85
Jealous

I am jealous for your heart. Do not let your heart be filled with troubles. Don't dwell on the things that can't be altered by you. Pray and move on, trusting in Me. I will intervene in My way and in My time. Fill your mind with glorious things, things which will build your faith. Choose to live with My joy. I will take care of you.

Let these verses encourage and direct you as you fill your heart with joy and peace:

Be anxious for nothing, but in everything by prayer and supplication, with thanksgiving, let your requests be made to God; and the peace of God, which surpasses all understanding, will guard your hearts and minds through Christ Jesus.
PHILIPPIANS 4:6-7

Finally, brethren, whatever things are true, whatever things are noble, whatever things are just, whatever things are pure, whatever things are lovely, whatever things are of good report, if there be any virtue and if there is anything praiseworthy—meditate on these things.
PHILIPPIANS 4:8

86
Your All-in-All

If you have a problem, I am the solution. If you lack wisdom, I am the teacher. Fear? I am your peace. Stress? I am your calm. Tired? I am your strength. I am your all-in-all. Just lean on Me and let go of the apprehensions you carry for the days ahead. I will give you My ease. I will order your steps and organize your days. Just give everything to Me.

What a wonderful God we have! He knows what we face in our day-to-day life. He understands our busy schedules, but nothing is too difficult for Him. He is our great Creator, so He can reveal creative ways for us to get everything done. We can trust Him to carry us through the "harried" times. I believe He not only wants us to get caught up but to do everything with excellence. So give Him your calendar, your planner, and your thoughts, and place your trust in Him.

> *Come to Me, all you who are heavy laden,*
> *and I will give you rest.*
> **MATTHEW 11:28**

> *Trust in the Lord with all your heart,*
> *And lean not on your own understanding;*
> *In all your ways acknowledge Him,*
> *And He shall direct your paths.*
> **PROVERBS 3:5-6**

87
His Mercy

. . . for His mercy endures forever.

This statement from Psalm 136 is repeated twenty-six times as a response to the start of each verse.

So what does *mercy* mean? *Webster's Dictionary* describes mercy as a show of leniency or divine blessing. For the Israelites during ancient biblical times, I'd say it was a little of both.

The psalmist talks about how God showed mercy to His people by creating the earth and the heavens, by giving the sun and moon to make the day and night, by bringing the Israelites out from Egypt, by dividing the Red Sea, and by giving them the Promised Land as a heritage, just to name a few. Obviously, the psalmist wants us to know that God's mercy endures forever.

Upon reading these words of Scripture, my eyes were drawn to the word *forever*. This means we can appropriate that leniency and divine blessing for ourselves.

This doesn't mean we can run around willy-nilly, sinning whenever we please, however. But we do know that when we stumble and fall, we have a loving Father who will be there when we repent, pick ourselves up, and dust ourselves off. He is always willing to forgive us and show us His mercy.

Knowing that stirs my heart! Psalm 103:8 says, "The Lord is merciful and gracious, slow to anger, and abounding in mercy." I'm so thankful for that. What a wonderful, gracious Father we have!

> *The steps of a good man are ordered by the Lord,*
> *And He delights in his way.*
> *Though he fall, he shall not be utterly cast down;*
> *For the Lord upholds him with His hand.*
> *I have been young, and now am old;*
> *Yet I have not seen the righteous forsaken,*
> *Nor his descendants begging bread.*
> *He is ever merciful, and lends;*
> *And his descendants are blessed.*
> **PSALM 37:23-26**

*And His mercy is on those who fear Him
From generation to generation.*
LUKE 1:50

88
Our Heritage

We often hear about people looking into their heritage, and there are even shows on PBS like *Finding Your Roots* and *Genealogy Roadshow* about people trying to find out about their ancestors and their past.

Do you ever wonder about your spiritual heritage? I have. I was reading the following Scripture that was spoken over my family a couple of years ago, and it's special to me:

> *"As for Me," says the Lord, "this is My covenant with them:*
> *My Spirit who is upon you, and My words which I have put in your*
> *mouth, shall not depart from your mouth, nor from the mouth of your*
> *descendants, nor from the mouth of your descendants' descendants,"*
> *says the Lord, "from this time and forevermore."*
> **Isaiah 59:21**

What a wonderful promise from a covenant-keeping God! I look at my children and grandchildren and know that they can benefit from this covenant that God made many generations ago.

As I've thought about what my spiritual heritage is, I realize that someone in my ancestral heritage was likely part of this covenant. Someone, moved in the Spirit, spoke God's Word to the next generation and created a spiritual heritage.

Some of us, though, can't think of even one godly ancestor. Maybe you feel like you are the only one who has chosen life in Him, but it's entirely possible that only one person before you who gave his or her life to the Lord and entered into this covenant. How thankful I am that someone in my family tree opened this opportunity for me and my descendants.

I am once again reminded of how important it is to make our children and grandchildren aware of this rich spiritual heritage we have. We must recount what God has done in our lives, recording our spiritual history for our descendants so they can pass that information along to the next generation.

> *Therefore, know that the Lord your God,*
> *He is God, the faithful God who keeps covenant and*
> *mercy for a thousand generations with those who*
> *love Him and keep His commandments.*
> **Deuteronomy 7:9**

*The Lord knows the days of the upright,
And their inheritance shall be forever.*
Psalm 37:18

89
He Keeps Us

During worship at our church, we sang a song about God never letting us go. The song's lyrics resonated with me, and I began thinking about what that meant for us. If He doesn't let us go, that means He *keeps* us. We are tethered to Him by His great love for us. The underlying message is that if we trust in Him, He will forever be our Keeper. What a glorious promise! What a gracious God!

Behold, I am with you and will keep you wherever you go.
Genesis 28:15a

Where can I go from Your Spirit?
Or where can I flee from Your presence?
If I ascend into heaven, You are there;
If I make my bed in hell, behold, You are there.
If I take the wings of the morning,
And dwell in the uttermost parts of the sea,
Even then Your right hand shall lead me,
And your right hand shall hold me.
Psalm 139:7-10

The Lord is your keeper;
The Lord is your shade at your right hand.
The sun shall not strike you by day,
Nor the moon by night.

The Lord shall preserve you from all evil;
He shall preserve your soul.
The Lord shall preserve your going out and your coming in
From this time forth, and even forevermore.
Psalm 121:5-8

90
Our God

I have been contemplating our amazing God. As I write this, I am overwhelmed by how good and great He is, and how blessed we are to call Him *our God*. This is how David put it in 1 Chronicles 29:10-13:

> "Blessed are You, Lord God of Israel,
> our Father, forever and ever.
> Yours, O Lord, is the greatness,
> The power and the glory,
> The victory and the majesty;
> For all that is in heaven and in earth is Yours;
> Yours is the kingdom, O Lord,
> And You are exalted as head over all.
> Both riches and honor come from You,
> And You reign over all.
> In Your hand is power and might;
> In Your hand it is to make great
> and to give strength to all.
>
> "Now, therefore, our God,
> We thank You
> And praise Your glorious name."

What have we done to deserve such a God? The answer is *nothing*, but His grace is extended to us every moment of every hour of every day. How can we not be grateful? How can we not rejoice?

He takes us with our weaknesses, our past lives, our stubborn wills, and He turns us upside down and inside out, creating new creatures. My heart sings! My feet dance! I celebrate this God who calls us His own.

Take time to give Him praise and thanksgiving, for He is worthy!

91
Grace

I have been contemplating God's grace, for which I am deeply grateful. His grace is His kindness toward us, His favor upon us. In the Bible concordance that I use, there are sixty-two references about *grace*.

That doesn't even include the references for *gracious*, which refers to God when He is pouring out His grace upon us. Just that alone shows us the importance of grace. As a good friend of mine would say, "It's a serious deal!"

Where would we be without grace? How do we get through even one day without God's acceptance of who we are? All I can say is that grace is priceless and yet is freely given to us. Ephesians 2:8 tells us that we wouldn't even be saved were it not for grace—a gift from God.

I love how Graham Cooke, a popular conference speaker on the topic of prophecy, talks about grace. He says that we don't have good days or bad days. Rather, each day is a "day of grace," which allows us to enjoy and celebrate some days and enables us to endure difficult days. Grace carries us through whatever life throws us. I love that! Each day is a day of grace, no matter what happens to us.

Here are a few verses on grace that really speak to me:

> And He said to me, "My grace is sufficient for you,
> for My strength is made perfect in weakness."
> **2 Corinthians 12:9**

> Let us therefore come boldly to the throne of grace,
> that we may obtain mercy and grace to help in time of need.
> **Hebrews 4:16**

> But He gives more grace. Therefore He says:
> "God resists the proud,
> But gives grace to the humble."
> **James 4:6**

> For the Lord God is a sun and shield.
> The Lord will give grace and glory.
> No good thing will He withhold
> From those who walk uprightly.
> **Psalm 84:11**

92
He Delights in Me

He delivered me because He delighted in me.
Psalm 18:19b

These words from one of the Psalms was written by David. Since his God is our God, the same testimony can be claimed by us.

My breath catches a little whenever I read this second part of Psalm 18:19, not just because He will deliver me, but because He *delights* in me. What a wonderful concept: *He delights in me!* Sure, I know He loves me, but it's another thing to know He delights in me.

Think of your children or other family members. You love them, but you don't always delight in them. According to this Scripture, however, God delivers us because He delights in us. To delight is to be "tickled" or be "thrilled." The thought of God feeling that way toward me causes an explosion of joy within!

I want to live my life hopelessly in love with Him. I want to show that love in my acts, my words, my thoughts, and even my countenance. I want to please Him and have Him delighted in me.

93
Ashes

Ashes may contain some slight heat but turn cold quickly. There is no comfort to be found in them. The ashes are easily blown away, and nothing is left, just emptiness. So it is with those who try to build their lives upon another "god." I am the only One who is the everlasting Comforter and lover of your soul. I will not be "blown away."

I am steadfast and sure—an anchor for your life.

After receiving this Word, I examined myself. Were there other "gods" or idols in my life? Was there something or someone in my life that had my complete attention at times? Does this "god" consume my thoughts?

A "god" in your life could be watching TV shows and sporting events, shopping, friendships, your job, making more money, fixing up your house, or even your hobbies. There is nothing inherently bad about any of these things—as long as they do not replace your time with God or take you away from reading His Word.

If there are other things always in the forefront of your mind, then it's hard to hear Him when He's talking to you. Be sure to listen to His Word. The things of this world are fleeting. They become as ashes. They are easily blown away on the winds of life.

The things of God, however, are eternal. They are our sure foundation. Jesus wants us to be remain His "first love," the one we think of when we wake up, the one we live for each day, and the one we pray to when we go to sleep at night. Everything and everyone comes after Him. He is worthy of having precedence in everything we do.

> *. . . we do not look at the things which*
> *are seen, but at the things which are not seen.*
> *For the things which are seen are temporary,*
> *but the things which are not seen are eternal.*
>
> **2 Corinthians 4:18**

> *Create in me a clean heart, O God,*
> *And renew a steadfast spirit within me.*
> *Do not cast me away from your presence,*
> *And do not take Your Holy Spirit from me.*
>
> *Restore to me the joy of your salvation,*
> *And uphold me by Your generous Spirit.*
>
> **Psalm 51:10-12**

94
God's Abundance

My love knows no bounds. My mercy flows freely to those who fear Me. My grace follows after those whom I have chosen. I am not a God of lack... but of abundance. There is no emptiness that I cannot fill. I own the cattle on a thousand hills. How could I not be a generous God to those I call My own? Rejoice this day in My abundance! Glory in My great love for you!

> *Surely goodness and mercy shall follow me*
> *All the days of my life;*
> *And I will dwell in the house of the Lord*
> *Forever.*
> **PSALM 23:6**

> *Now to Him who is able to do exceedingly abundantly above all that we ask or think, according to the power that works in us, to Him be glory in the church by Christ Jesus to all generations, forever and ever. Amen.*
> **EPHESIANS 3:20-21**

> *Bless the Lord, O my soul;*
> *And all that is within me, bless His holy name!*
> *Bless the Lord, O my soul,*
> *And forget not all His benefits.*
> **PSALM 103:1-2**

What a gracious God!

What a generous God!

What a good God!

95
Get in the Word

Find strength in My Word. Find peace in My Word. Fill yourself with its promises and its wisdom. Measure your thoughts and actions by My Word. It is truly the "Sword of the Spirit," the weapon that can defeat the enemy. Read and be encouraged and prepared for each day.

I was reading Psalm 139 and was greatly encouraged by verse 5:

You have hedged me behnd and before,
And laid Your hand upon me.

Picture this! God has our back while going before us and shielding us from anything that will come our way. On top of that, His hand is always on us. How awesome is that? Then these verses (17-18) from Psalm 139 stood out to me:

How precious also are Your thoughts to me, O God!
How great is the sum of them!
If I should count them, they would be more in number than the sand;
When I awake, I am still with You.

Sometimes we say to people, "I'll be thinking of you." How long and how often do we really think about them after saying that? If you're like me, not that much. We get distracted and we forget. We're human. But God's thoughts are *always* toward us. He is faithful! Just knowing that strengthens my faith, encourages me, and brings me peace.

I suggest reading all of Psalm 139. You'll be encouraged and blessed!

96
A Covering

There was a Band-Aid commercial on TV that closed with the jingle, "Covering is caring." I couldn't get that jingle out of my mind for days—or the words behind it.

Before turning in, parents check their little ones to make sure they are *covered* in their beds. When a loved one falls asleep on the couch, you *cover* them with a throw blanket so that they will be comfortable. Sometimes you *cover* for a fellow worker if he or she has an emergency. You might tell a friend, "I have it *covered*," which means that you will take care of the situation—and he or she doesn't have to worry.

Covering is a sign of love, of tenderness, of caring. Now when the Band-Aid commercial comes to mind, I can't help but think of Jesus when the jingle "Covering is caring" hums in my head. He *covered* for us when He went to the cross. When we receive Him as our Lord and Savior, He *covers* us with a robe of righteousness. He continues to *cover* us with His love, His favor, and His grace. He tells us not to worry because He "has it *covered*."

When I am seeking His face in my quiet time, I feel His presence *cover* Me like a soft blanket of love, which soothes and comforts me. How precious to be *covered* by Him!

> **Blessed is he whose transgression if forgiven,**
> **Whose sin in covered.**
> **PSALM 32:1**

> **Egypt was glad when they departed,**
> **For the fear of them had fallen upon them.**
> **He spread a cloud for a covering,**
> **And fire to give light in the night.**
> **PSALM 105:38-39**

> **He shall cover you with His feathers,**
> **And under His wings you shall take refuge.**
> **PSALM 91:4A**

97
Happy Feet

I have a son-in-law who is a great cook and a real foodie. When he eats something especially good, he often says, "Happy feet! Happy feet!", meaning he feels like dancing because of the enjoyable eating experience.

If he eats a meal prepared by me and says, "Happy feet!", then I know I've hit the mark. This reminds me of Psalm 34:8, which says, "Oh, taste and see that the Lord is good." The Lord is truly good. I might even say delicious!

When I worship Him, I love to dance. There are times when He is so wonderful that I want to abandon myself to Him and dance with "happy feet."

God not only gives us "happy feet," but He gives us feet that dance on the high places. Consider this verse:

> *The Lord God is my strength;*
> *He will make my feet like deer's feet,*
> *And He will make me walk on my high hills.*
> **HABAKKUK 3:19**

Deer are among the most sure-footed of all mountain animals. How wonderful that God gives us steady feet as we climb some of life's precarious "mountains."

God also blesses our feet with strength in battle:

> *For by You I can run against a troop,*
> *By my God I can leap over a wall.*
> **PSALM 18:29-30**

God gives us the ability to escape the enemy! He allows us to be lifted up, so as you face "mountains" in your day, think of all the provisions God has given to you and how gracious and generous He is.

98
Glory in Me

Glory in Me! Dance in Me! Sing in Me! Let your spirit rise. Don't be willing to settle for anything less than Me. Always keep your eyes on the heavenlies. Soar with Me. As you walk through the daily circumstances, keep your heart and mind fixed on Me. I will be your "secret weapon." The enemy will not be able to pull you into discouragement or despair. You will dance above his grasp and confound him with your praise.

This Word lifts my spirit and makes me smile. Isn't God good? He always knows what we need. He loves to watch us dance and sing in Him. He helps us to get our heads on straight and our attitudes in line.

I love to worship Him. I love being in His presence. I love that our praise and worship sets the enemy on his ear.

Make a joyful shout to God, all the earth!
Sing out the honor of His name;
Make His name glorious.
PSALM 66:1-2

Let Israel rejoice in their Maker;
Let the children of Zion be joyful in their King.
Let them praise His name with the dance;
Let them sing praises to Him with the timbrel and harp.
For the Lord takes pleasure in His people;
He will beautify the humble with salvation.
PSALM 149:2-4

99
God of Comfort

Come here, My beloved. Lay your head upon My chest. Rest in Me and receive all that I have for you. Your heart is wounded, and you are losing hope. You are safe with Me. I have everything under control. Don't act out of fear or anger or pride. Let go, and let Me handle this. Keep your eyes on Me, not the circumstances. I am growing you.

I'm so thankful for the unconditional love that God offers continuously. He is always there with grace and mercy overflowing. I trust God to carry me through.

> *Deep calls unto deep at the noise of Your waterfalls;*
> *All Your waves and billows have gone over me.*
> *The Lord will command His lovingkindness in the daytime,*
> *And in the night His song shall be with me—*
> *A prayer to the God of my life.*
> **Psalm 42:7-8**

> *Grace, mercy, and peace will be with you from*
> *God the Father and from the Lord Jesus Christ,*
> *the Son of the Father, in truth and love.*
> **2 John 1:3**

100
Extend Grace

My grace is sufficient for you. There is no limit. I pour it out freely to those who know Me. You walk in My grace, live in My grace, and breathe in My grace, which is an expression of My love for you. Soak it in, and in turn, give grace to others. Be gracious as you deal with those around you. Stir up their hunger for Me by extending grace to them.

Sometimes I would tell my students that I was giving them grace when they didn't deserve it. Maybe they got recess even though they had lost it because of poor behavior. Maybe they got a deadline extended for an assignment even though they had plenty of time to complete the project. When those things happened, I explained that grace was a favor given to them even though it wasn't deserved. I gave them grace because I loved them.

As adults, we need to look for ways to extend grace to others in our daily lives. Maybe the next time you're standing in the express lane at the grocery store, and the lady in front of you has fifty items in her cart. Okay, maybe I exaggerate, but there are sure more than a dozen items in her cart. You could put her on the spot and tell her she's in the express lane—or you could extend grace and give her a warm smile and a friendly greeting.

You have no idea what she's going through or what her life is like. Maybe she's about to be laid off at work and is not thinking clearly. Maybe there's an emergency in her family, and she needs to get through the line quickly.

Or consider this: What if she is just being rude and selfish? What then? How many times has our attitude or behavior been less than perfect? And yet, God forgives and pours out His grace. Do the same for her.

Remember, we show God's love by giving people the benefit of the doubt and extending grace. Doing so reveals that our heart is in line with God's heart, and that pleases the Father.

*And He said to me, "My grace is sufficient for you,
for My strength is made perfect in weakness."*
2 Corinthians 12:9a

*But God, who is rich in mercy, because of His great love
with which He loved us, even when we were dead in trespasses,
made us alive together with Christ (by grace you have been saved),
and raised us up together, and made us sit together in the
heavenly places in Christ Jesus, that in the ages to come
He might show the exceeding riches of His grace in
His kindness toward us in Christ Jesus.*

EPHESIANS 2:4-7

101
Claim the Promises

Claim the promises. You have the right as My children. Pull on your rightful inheritance. Claim My Word. Speak it over yourself and your loved ones. Write it down. Slip it into your purse or pocket. Take it with you wherever you go, as a reminder. Put it on your walls, your refrigerator, your mirror. Look upon My Word and claim its promises throughout the day. It will give you strength. It will give you direction. It will ground you when the rest of the world is constantly shifting and changing. My Word is eternal. I am held to My Word.

I love God's Word, and I am grateful for the promises that I find in it. Here are a few promises I hold dear:

> *For He Himself has said, "I will never leave you nor forsake you."*
> **HEBREWS 13:5B**

> *"Call to Me, and I will answer you, and show you great and mighty things, which you do not know."*
> **JEREMIAH 33:3**

> *Surely goodness and mercy shall follow me*
> *All the days of my life.*
> **PSALM 23:6A**

> *"As for Me," says the Lord, "this is My covenant with them: My Spirit who is upon you, and My words which I have put in your mouth, shall not depart from your mouth, nor from the mouth of your descendants, nor from the mouth of your descendants' descendants," says the Lord, "from this time and forevermore."*
> **ISAIAH 59:21**

What promises are special to you? Think on those today, and be encouraged.

102
Moment-by-Moment God

Change is hard! Can you relate? Jobs change. Family dynamics change. Neighbors change. Our bodies change. I, personally, have experienced a lot of those things. I've given myself a "pity party" because of them.

But God is faithful! The last time I was feeling mopey, He interrupted my pity party and gave Me this Word:

I will not allow you to be cast adrift. I am your anchor. You are not without resource. I am your answer. You are not left alone. I am your steadfast ally. Do not let your circumstances alter your view of Me. I am the one true God. I will not be changed. I am the same yesterday, today, and forever. There is no shadow of turning with Me. I can do ALL THINGS. I meet you wherever your need is. There is nothing too trivial, nothing that is too "earthly" for Me to intervene. I want to be your moment-by-moment God. Look to Me and cast your cares upon me. I am here and I am now. Give Me your today and trust Me with your tomorrow.

What a mighty, gracious, merciful, and good God we have!

He who did not spare His own Son,
but delivered Him up for us all, how shall
He not with Him also freely give us all things?
ROMANS 8:32

103
Examine Yourself

Examine yourself. What are your priorities? Ask the Holy Spirit to reveal them to you.

What is your passion? Family? Job? Sports? Fashion? Music? Food? There is nothing wrong with any of these. However, whatever consumes your time and your thoughts can control your life.

I am calling you to a higher level. I am calling you to a deeper relationship with Me. The days are coming when those with a shallow faith will be swept away. The ones left standing will be those who stand firmly on the Rock—their true passion.

The first thought that came to mind after receiving this Word was the story of the man who built his house on the rock (Luke 6:48). He dug deep and laid his foundation on stone. The house was strong and withstood a flood since it was founded on rock.

The world buffets us daily like an unrelenting torrent of water, threatening to destroy us. So, what do we do? I say we look toward God. To know Him is to love Him. To love Him means we want to please Him.

We need to see Him as the One who sits above the circle of the earth, ruling over all (Isaiah 40:22). We need to see Him high and lifted up as the train of His robe fills the temple (Isaiah 6:1) We need to see Him sending His Son to the Cross to die for us. We need to see Him as Abba—Daddy God.

How can we ignore His call to a deeper relationship with Him? I want to dig deep and lay my foundation on Him. I want to stand strong for Him.

In closing, I have always liked the old-time worship song, "Turn Your Eyes Upon Jesus," written in 1922 by Helen H. Lemmel. Even today, the song's message is still current:

> *Turn your eyes upon Jesus.*
> *Look full in His wonderful face,*
> *And the things of earth will grow strangely dim,*
> *In the light of His glory and grace.*

To which I say, "Amen!"

104
Don't Wait

Don't wait until your heart is faint before you come to Me. Don't wait until your head is bent low and your spirit is weary. Come daily; come moment-by-moment. Be restored.

Remember the Rock pours oil of refreshment upon you. My waters renew your spirit. I am the lifter of your head. This does not mean you have to be low in order to be lifted. I can lift your head and keep it lifted. It is My desire. Just turn your eyes in My direction, and I will gladly rush to you.

And the rock poured out rivers of oil for me!
Job 29:6b

But, You, O Lord, are a shield for me,
My glory and the One who lifts up my head.
Psalm 3:3

I am determined to keep my eyes on the One who lifts my head. Only He can calm me and keep things in perspective.

105
Every Day

Every day is a step closer to the end. This might sound simplistic, but My words need to be seriously considered. What are you doing with each day? Do you begin your morning by thinking, *I can't wait until this day is over*? Or do you savor every minute? Do you look for "God moments"?

Make the most of each day because you don't know if you will have tomorrow. Keep your eyes and heart tuned in to Me.

I'm thinking of all the opportunities I've missed in a day because my thoughts were carried away by other things.

I would imagine that you feel the same way, but every day, there are opportunities to be a light to others. If you're at a grocery store, look for someone to encourage, even if it's only a smile or a kind word.

I remember the time when my daughters and I were in a supermarket in Omaha. It was 10:30 at night. We met another Christian while pushing our shopping carts and ended up having a great conversation, followed by prayer, right there in the store aisle. At work or at home, there are many people who just need a warm smile, a hug, and perhaps prayer.

When you're driving a car, you can redeem the time by praying and praising God. Go ahead—be loud! I have had some of My most profound moments with God while driving to my next errand, so remember this:

> *This is the day the Lord has made;*
> *We will rejoice and be glad in it.*
> **Psalm 118:24**

106
Enriched

The word *enriched* has been rolling around in my head. I finally realized that this is what God wanted me to write about, so here we go.

When I learned that *enrich* means "to make richer or more productive," I looked up *rich* as well. Besides meaning "wealthy," *rich* also connotes something "of great value; satisfying and pleasing." When we look at a food product label, and it says "enriched," we know something has been added to make the food better or more satisfying.

"Enriched" applies to our lives when the Lord is an integral part. Our lives become fuller and richer when He enters. We no longer have to struggle under the weight of sin. His love is poured out upon us. We become the "apple of His eye," His favorite one, and His beloved.

Goodness and mercy follow us all of our days. He protects us and rescues us. He gives us the mind of Christ and wisdom when we ask. The Lord prepares good works that we might walk in them. He sees us as righteous. We are filled with all the fullness of God.

I could go on and on. What a privilege to be His! I feel truly satisfied and of great value by knowing Him. Take time to reflect on what it means to have Him in your life.

> *Now to Him Who, by (in consequence of) the [action of His] power that is at work within us, is able to [carry out His purpose and] do superabundantly, far over and above all that we [dare] ask or think [infinitely beyond our highest prayers, desires, thoughts, hopes, or dreams]—To Him be glory in the church and in Christ Jesus throughout all generations forever and ever. Amen (so be it).*
> **Ephesians 3:20-21, Amplified Bible, Classic Edition**

107
Encourage Yourself

Our lovely neighbor moved away. Then at school, our principal, whom we love and respect, took a new position outside of the district. Some teachers I'd known for a long time were also leaving the school, and there were people in our church who were leaving our city.

These changes were disheartening. As I considered all these moves, I received this Word from the Lord:

I have spoken to you about changes and disruptions in your life. I remind you again that I am your Rock. The bottom line is: DO YOU TRUST ME?

People weave in and out of your life, leaving deposits of themselves. Be thankful for those deposits and move forward. Every disappointment is an opportunity to bring glory to Me. Live above the circumstances because the Almighty God has His hand on you, and the Holy Spirit leads and guides you continually. You are My people. Be set apart by how you respond in these situations. Allow My peace to fill you.

> *Why are you cast down, O my soul?*
> *And why are you disquieted within me?*
> *Hope in God;*
> *For I shall yet praise Him,*
> *The help of my countenance, and my God.*
>
> **Psalm 42:11**

In this psalm, King David spoke to his own soul, encouraging himself by remembering the times God had rescued him and blessed him. In the same way, we need to put the future in God's hands and let Him know we trust Him in all things.

108
Empty Things

I was reading in 1 Samuel where Samuel was admonishing the people of Israel concerning their wickedness. The following section is what struck me:

> *"... yet do not turn aside from following the Lord, but serve the Lord with all your heart. And do not turn aside; for then you would go after empty things which cannot profit or deliver, for they are nothing."*
> **1 Samuel 12:20b-21**

The *empty things* caught my attention because according to the Lord, things that are not profitable are empty.

Was I spending my time on "empty things"? I knew there were harmless things that did not have eternal value like reading a good novel, watching a movie, playing a sport, going shopping, or chatting with friends or family. In essence, though, these are not bad things.

I think the point of this Scripture is the part about serving the Lord with all your heart. In other words, are we also spending time with the Lord? Are we in prayer? Are we reading His Word? Are we attending church? Are we ministering to others? Are we feeding the hungry and clothing the poor? Are we reaching out to the outcasts, the lonely, and the less fortunate? Are we doing work on behalf of the kingdom? Are we spending the majority of our time on things that make an impact eternally?

I think the key is balance and always keeping ourselves in check. We don't want all of our accomplishments in this life to end up burned as hay and stubble. In the end, we want the Lord to say about this about our lives: "Well done, good and faithful servant" (Matthew 25:21).

I'm not talking about "works" here but being sensitive to the Lord and letting Him lead and guide us so that we may please and glorify Him while we walk this earth.

> *"For the Lord will not forsake His people, for His great name's sake because it has pleased the Lord to make you His people. Only fear the Lord, and serve Him in truth with all your heart; for consider what great things He has done for you."*
> **1 Samuel 12:22,24**

> *Turn away my eyes from looking at worthless things,*
> *And revive me in Your way.*
> **Psalm 119:37**

109
Come Away

Come away! Come away! Come away from your tasks. Come away from the office, the gym, the kitchen, and the book you are reading. Come away a little while, just to gaze upon Me. Let yourself be refreshed, restored, and renewed. Be wrecked in My presence. Be ruined for the things of this world, and be desperate for Me.

How He loves us! How He longs for us! He is a jealous God. He won't settle for a sideways glance at Him or a quick scan of His Word. He wants our undivided attention. Isn't He worthy of that?

I know our lives are busy. I know we are pulled on every side. He just wants our best effort to be with Him. If we are willing, He will work out a way. We will be all the better for making the effort. We will be better prepared for the day set before us.

> *Come to Me, all you who labor and*
> *are heavy laden, and I will give you rest.*
> **MATTHEW 11:28**

> *In Your presence is fullness of joy;*
> *At your right hand pleasures forevermore.*
> **PSALM 16:11B**

> *Let all those who seek You rejoice and be glad in You.*
> **PSALM 40:16A**

> *Be still, and know that I am God.*
> **PSALM 46:10A**

110
Comfort Others

We lost my mom a few years ago. After a few weeks, I went up to Minnesota to visit my dad and see how he was doing. Our time together was good but difficult. I also met old acquaintances and saw people at my old church that I hadn't seen for a long time.

The wonderful thing was the listening ears and words of advice about dealing with an elderly parent. Advice from someone who has already walked through what you are facing is priceless.

It made me think of the body of Christ and how we should be God's hand extended, not only to one another, but to those outside of the Church. We carry the Comforter, and we know He desires for us to minister to others. We are His agents of love. Kind words and acts of comfort are precious to those in need.

> *Blessed be the God and Father of our Lord Jesus Christ, the Father of mercies and God of all comfort, who comforts us in all our tribulation, so that we may be able to comfort those who are in any trouble, with the comfort with which we ourselves are comforted by God.*
> **2 CORINTHIANS 1:3-4**

> *Pleasant words are like a honeycomb, Sweetness to the soul and health to the bones.*
> **PROVERBS 16:24**

> *And a word spoken in due season, how good it is!*
> **PROVERBS 15:23B**

111
Rich Cream

T hose who know me well know that I love coffee. I especially like my coffee with cream. Not just half-and-half, but heavy cream. Cream adds a richness. Cream enhances the flavor of the coffee. Cream lightens the color of the coffee and creates a smooth, delicious treat. Don't worry: I *am* going somewhere with this.

I was reading in the Book of Job where Job was talking about how he wished he could go back to how things were before all of the calamities had occurred in his life. In Job 29:2-6, he describes the ways in which God had blessed his life:

Oh, that I were as in months past,
As in the days when God watched over me;
When His lamp shone upon my head,
And when by His light I walked through darkness;
Just as I was in my prime,
When the friendly counsel of God was over my tent;
When the Almighty was yet with me,
When my children were around me;
When my steps were bathed in cream,
And the rock poured out rivers of oil for me!

These are the same benefits that we can expect and enjoy when we walk with Him. I want Him watching over me, shining upon my head and lighting the darkness. How wonderful to have His counsel over us. Our steps being bathed with cream, and rivers of oil poured over us show what an abundant and gracious God He is! He is not stingy! He will not give us half-and-half when we can have rich, heavy cream.

How precious is Your lovingkindness, O God!
Therefore the children of men put their trust under the shadow of Your wings.
They are abundantly satisfied with the fullness of Your house,
And You give them drink from the river of Your pleasures.
Psalm 36:7-8

112
Chosen

I have been thinking about the word "chosen." If you've been chosen for a special award or tribute, you feel elated. If you're married, your spouse chose you over all the others to be your life-long partner. Pretty special!

Then there's the other side of the coin. A bunch of kids on the playground are choosing up teams. One after another, kids are picked. As they run off to play, you realize you weren't chosen. Feelings of inadequacy, loneliness, and isolation take over. Or when you were older, as an adult, maybe you weren't chosen for a new position in the company or were passed over for a promotion.

We've all experienced similar situations: it's a part of life, a part of growing up and maturing. But as believers in Jesus, we have good news! WE WERE CHOSEN! Yes, God chose us before the foundation of the world (Ephesians 1:4). In Jeremiah 1:5, God's Word says He knew us even before we were born. Amazing!

Because we were chosen, we have value in the eyes of the chooser. We can rest in the fact that God looks into us and sees us as valuable and precious. That should make us feel elated!

Here are some more verses to encourage you as His chosen one:

> *Blessed is the man You choose,*
> *And cause to approach You,*
> *That he may dwell in Your courts.*
> *We shall be satisfied with the goodness of Your house,*
> *Of Your holy temple.*
> **Psalm 65:4**

> *Remember His marvelous works which He has done,*
> *His wonders, and the judgments of His mouth,*
> *O seed of Abraham His servant,*
> *You children of Jacob, His chosen ones.*
> **Psalm 105:5-6**

Remember me, O Lord, with the favor You have toward Your people.
Oh, visit me with Your salvation.
That I may see the benefit of Your chosen ones,
That I may rejoice in the gladness of Your nation,
That I may glory with Your inheritance.

Psalm 106:4-5

A Closing Thought
by Senior Pastor Dave Olson

The Lord will often bring gifted people into our lives to reveal what is available to the rest of us. They are intended not only to instruct us but also provoke us to hunger. Now that you have read *His Heart, His Voice*, I want to let you in on a secret: God wants to speak to you with the same clarity.

I have found, however, that hearing God is similar to hearing a compliment: it's often easier to receive for others than it is for ourselves. It is for this reason that I encourage you to revisit the content of this book often. Allow Linda's devotional thoughts to familiarize you with God's heart toward you. Let her words recalibrate your view of Him and perhaps more importantly, His view of you.

But don't stop there. Set aside your own time for daily hearing. Find a place that becomes your shared place with God. Have your Bible as well as a pen and paper handy.

Begin by reading His Word as your personal letter. Then, with pen in hand, quiet your heart and ask Him if there is anything specific He would like to say to you. You will be pleasantly surprised at how talkative God is.

I discovered early on in my walk with God that He loves to speak to us. The things He's showed me personally have been the most substantial to me. Journal what He shows you and become the "ready writer" of Psalm 45:1.

I promise you will find yourself returning to reread what He has spoken to you, and you will be encouraged and edified.

Dave Olson is the senior pastor of Heartland Church in Ankeny, Iowa.

About the Author

Linda Daniels grew up in Jackson, Minnesota, a small farming community in the southwestern corner of the state.

Upon graduation from high school, Linda attended Morningside College in Sioux City, Iowa, where she majored in elementary education. While in college, she met her future husband, Ron. They married after their sophomore year, and their first child, Marc, was born during their senior year.

In 1971, Linda graduated and began teaching. In her first year in the classroom, a co-worker witnessed to her and led her to the Lord. Their family began attending church. Three years later, twin girls, Megan and Erin, made their family complete.

Teaching was Linda's passion. She taught in various Midwest locations—Sioux City, Des Moines, and Davenport in Iowa and Omaha, Nebraska—because the company Ron worked for transferred him several times. Except for times she didn't teach because of moves or having babies, Linda spent thirty-seven years in the classroom until she retired in 2016.

A few years before retirement, God began changing her passion. She and Ron were attending Heartland Church in Ankeny, Iowa. God was growing and stretching her spiritually. She became a part of the altar ministry team, the prophetic team, and an intercessory prayer group. Her passion for teaching was changed to a passion for ministry. That led to experiences in prison ministry and street evangelism. While at Heartland Church, Linda earned her ministry credentials from Heartland Alliance.

Following God's leading, Ron and Linda moved to Omaha, where their children and ten grandchildren live. Linda continues in intercessory prayer and ministry. Whether praying, mentoring, or speaking, Linda's desire is to bring others into an encounter with the Lord so that they may find their destiny in Him.

Invite Linda Daniels to Speak Today

Linda Daniels is a thoughtful speaker with a passion to talk about how God's Word is alive today and offers comfort, encouragement, peace, and direction. She is available to speak at various church gatherings as well as weekend women's retreats.

If you, your community group, women's ministry, or church would be interested in having Linda speak at your event, please contact her through her email address at sosgodskisses@gmail.com.